HMS BOUNTY

By the same author

THE COAL-SCUTTLE BRIGADE
BLACK SATURDAY
STRIKE FROM THE SKY
THE GOLDEN WRECK
HMS BOUNTY
THE FRIENDLESS SKY
FROM MERCILESS INVADERS
CAEN: ANVIL OF VICTORY
GORDON OF KHARTOUM
VIMY RIDGE
FARMING THE SEA
HISTORY UNDER THE SEA
THE RACE FOR THE RHINE BRIDGES
KING HENRY VIII'S MARY ROSE
DEATH RAFT
THE QUEEN'S CORSAIR
ICE CRASH
INTO THE BLUE
DRESDEN: THE DEVIL'S TINDERBOX
HOW WE FOUND THE MARY ROSE
TARQUIN'S SHIP
THE MOSQUITO LOG
A HERITAGE OF SHIPS

HMS BOUNTY

A True Account of the Notorious Mutiny

ALEXANDER McKEE

SOUVENIR PRESS

First Published 1961 under the title
The Truth about the Mutiny on the Bounty

This edition first published 1989 by Souvenir Press Ltd,
43 Great Russell Street, London WC1B 3PA
and simultaneously in Canada

ISBN 0 285 62886 0

Printed and bound in Great Britain by
WBC Ltd, Bristol and Maesteg

Contents

(Map pages 136 and 137)

". . . there was no settled SYSTEM of Tyranny exercised by him likely to produce dissatisfaction. It was in those violent TORNADOS of temper when he lost himself."—CAPTAIN GEORGE TOBIN

1
Breadfruit and Cheese

THERE was a storm coming. The grey, December seas, white-capped, surged remorselessly into the great anchorage of Spithead. To the north, above the shallows of the triangular Spit Sand, the waves broke and fought in a choppy fury. To the south, the submerged bank known as No Man's Land was white with contesting seas. Drifts of bitter rain swept across the three miles of deep water that separated the two vast sandbanks. This deep water, shielded to the north by Portsmouth and the mainland, to the south by the Isle of Wight and to the west by both combined, was the main base of the British home fleet. In time of war, it was also a gathering place for the convoys of merchant ships which Britain regularly sent out across the world. In the very centre of the anchorage, a turmoil of angry water boiled around a sunken obstruction, from which three spray-stained masts reared up at a crazy angle. The wreck, still a hazard to navigation although it had sunk more than five years before, was that of the great line-of-battle ship *Royal George,* whose rotten bottom had fallen out of her. Some of the 800 men, women, and children who had gone down with her were still in the dark, weed-stained hull. Later, divers were to find, irrevocably entwined, the remnants of two cloaks—one of a woman, the other of a little girl—who had died locked in each other's arms as the great vessel heeled over and plunged to the bottom. It was usual for women and children to visit the ships as they lay out at Spithead, because, in many cases, the captains did not allow their crews ashore for fear of desertion. These were the unsuccessful captains—who rarely gained prize money for themselves or their men—or the few tyrants, whose rule under the strict laws of the sea could turn a warship into a hell afloat.

There had already been desertions from one of the ships now tossing under bare poles in the anchorage. Most of them were pressed men who had escaped while she was off Deptford, in the Thames, and before she had come round to Spithead. She was an unusual-looking ship—out of place in that gathering of warships—and her mission was unusual, too. Her destination was the South Seas, specifically Tahiti—or Otaheite, as it was then called. Her crew could hardly believe that they would soon be leaving behind them the cold and damp of an English winter, exchanging it for a golden paradise where blue, lazy waters creamed on a coral shore under a Pacific sun. She was barely large enough for the task which had been set her; accommodation was cramped, even by warship standards; but still, she was a new ship, and very well fitted out, with a copper bottom—the very latest thing in anti-corrosion devices—and all iron fastenings in the hull had been replaced by copper fastenings. On the other hand, the Admiralty had economised on pay by appointing to her only one commissioned officer—and a lieutenant at that. She carried as her figurehead the carving of a woman in a riding habit. Obviously a merchant ship, she looked even stranger because of the stumpiness of her masts—which had been cropped in order to increase her seaworthiness—and she was stranger still inside.

The whole of the main cabin aft, which was unusually well ventilated—with two large sky-lights and six scuttles—had a false deck with regular rows of holes in it. Below was a narrow space above the real deck, which was covered by a sheath of lead, and at one point a number of pipes led downwards to the deck below. In a ship of the eighteenth century Navy, this looked like Science Fiction. In reality, it was Science Fact. The rows of holes in the false deck were to take garden pots; the lead sheathing of the real deck was to prevent the fresh water leaking through onto the deck below; and the pipes were designed to draw off that water into large tubs, from where it could be taken again for the periodic watering of the plants. In effect, the ship was a floating conservatory, and there were indeed two botanists among the crew. But there were no plants in the garden pots as yet. They were to be collected from the Society Islands in the Pacific, where they grew in profusion, and transported by this ship to the West Indies, where it was hoped they would flourish, and provide a cheap and ample diet for the slaves who provided the main labour force for the plantations. The plant was the breadfruit, which grew on a tree about the size of an apple tree. The notoriety which subsequently attended the story of the voyage—the captain's account of it became a runaway "Best Seller"—led to his being given the nickname, inevitable in the circumstances, of "Breadfruit Bligh".

The ship was His Majesty's armed vessel *Bounty*—ex-*Bethia,* 215 tons—which had been bought by the Admiralty for £1,950, and specially refitted at Deptford for £4,456. Her new name was intended as a compliment to King George III for his interest in this scientific expedition, which had the support of the Royal Society. Having just lost their American colonies the British now, in 1787, were seeking to exploit their other interests and, in particular, those resulting from the preliminary probes into the Pacific—almost as remote then as is Outer Space today. Captain Cook was the legendary name of Pacific navigation and William Bligh had been chosen for command of the *Bounty,* partly because his wife's uncle was a man of some importance in the West Indies trade, but mainly because he had sailed as navigator and surveyor in the *Resolution* with Cook on his last expedition. The odd thing was that, very probably, if it had not been for the hasty temper of William Bligh, Captain Cook would have been alive still.

When Cook went ashore in Hawaii to remonstrate with the chiefs about thefts by the natives, two boats were left in the bay to prevent canoes escaping; one commanded by Lieutenant Rickman, the other by Bligh. A chief tried to get away in a canoe, both boats fired, and the chief was killed. When the news reached the natives on the beach, they attacked and killed Cook. This sequence of events was testified to, independently, by Captain Clerke, Cook's second-in-command, Lieutenants King and Burney, Mr. Edgar, the master of the *Resolution*, and William Bayley, an astronomer aboard the *Resolution*. Bligh was one of the two culprits, and his account was a masterpiece of evasion: "Lieut. Rickman did fire, and it was said killed a man; but the attack (on Cook) was over and past before that was known." The blame for firing Bligh put on Rickman; the chief he described as a "man"; his death he tried to pass off as rumour; and he altered the time of firing to after the death of Cook instead of before, so that no blame could possibly be attached to himself.

On this new voyage to the Pacific in the wake of Captain Cook, and even during his subsequent privations, Bligh kept a careful log. But he was not the only person on board to do so. James Morrison, the boatswain's mate, an educated man holding a position far below his station, also kept a journal from the start of the voyage—and what is more, managed to preserve it through a mutiny, a shipwreck, and a long open boat voyage.* John Fryer, the ship's master, subsequently wrote an account of what transpired, but, unlike Bligh's nar-

* It has been suggested (Rolf Du Rietz) that this was written after Morrison's return to England in 1792 and is not therefore a diary.

rative, it was not a best seller—for it was not even published. One of the Midshipmen, Peter Heywood, who survived court martial for mutiny, told his side of the story in a number of letters and in evidence at the court martial. Fletcher Christian, the leader of the mutiny, who disappeared without trace from a remote Pacific island on which he had taken refuge—although Heywood thought he saw him later in England—gave his own version to others, who repeated it. And there was a great deal of evidence given at the court martial by many other men, speaking as eyewitnesses of the extraordinary events which they described. What they did not mention, naturally enough, were the everyday facts of naval life which everyone knew and therefore took for granted. But those facts, too, are on record.

Portsmouth in the 1960s had a strangely forlorn air. There were hardly any warships in the harbour. In place of the impressive fleet of battleships stationed there before the Second World War, there were now only a handful of destroyers and frigates, a few cruisers armed with guns. When a really modern and formidable warship entered, it was invariably American—a guided-missile cruiser or nuclear submarine. By the 1980s, the fleet had shrunk further—and the gun-armed cruisers had gone, mostly to the breakers, but one for display in the Thames by the Tower of London as a museum ship. Indeed, a substantial part of the Portsmouth Naval Base had become a Heritage Area, with the greatest show of museum ships in the world, led by three battleships—Henry VIII's *Mary Rose* of 1509, Nelson's HMS *Victory* of 1765, and the first iron, armoured capital ship, HMS *Warrior* of 1860. Admittedly, by 1986 the Royal Navy had been modernised and was up to date, but also it had continued shrinking. From a 1960s strength of 95,000 men it had fallen to 56,820 male officers and ratings, plus some Wrens.

It is hard to recapture the atmosphere of the late eighteenth and nineteenth centuries, when Britain had the most powerful and victorious navy in the world, although—with a population of ten million—her enemies often outnumbered her three and four to one. In 1802 the underpopulated island was maintaining a vast fleet manned by 129,000 men. One hundred and ninety years later the same island, now desperately overpopulated, with more than fifty-five million people, has a navy of less than half that of 1802. Even so, there is a naval manning problem.

The background to Bligh and the mutiny of the *Bounty* can be coldly stated in black and white, in the figures for naval recruitment and losses for the war period 1774 to 1780:

Men raised	175,990
Killed in action	1,243
Lost by sickness	18,541
Loss by desertion ("Run")	42,069

The number of men enlisted was enormous, when compared to the resources of the country, and when it is remembered that most of them were seamen of one sort or another. The number killed in battle was minute, when compared to a land engagement, because in the latter case the guns were firing at masses of men, whereas in the former they were firing at masses of wood. The losses by sickness and disease were heavy and inevitable, because a warship was literally crammed with men, because medical knowledge was insufficient, and because there was no way on a long voyage of preventing the food and the drinking water from going bad. The loss by desertion was fantastic because the men had two main complaints—Pay and Leave. Brutality—the Navy was brutal—was not objected to; bad food—and it was inconceivably bad, crawling with worms and maggots—was not objected to. All these conditions obtained also in the merchant ships; and in a merchant ship the work was much harder, for the crews were small, whereas in a warship the men who in action worked the guns formed at all other times a very large reserve of labour.

What the seamen did object to were the poor rates of Naval pay (unchanged since the time of Cromwell), plus the method by which shore agents collected a rake-off on it, and the fact that, generally speaking, the Navy rarely gave leave to seamen—only to officers. This was not class distinction, merely tacit acceptance of the fact that, if they set foot on shore, the Navy was unlikely to see them again—at any rate, of their own free will. Therefore, a vicious circle was set up—the men deserting at the first opportunity because they were denied leave, and the Navy denying them leave because they were liable to desert. Worse still, the only way out of naval service was by wounds, sickness, or death. "I think it incontrovertible that *nothing* will induce, or encourage seamen to enter voluntarily on board of the Royal Fleet; but knowing the term of their servitude," wrote Lieutenant Tomlinson in 1774.

The Navy's deficiencies in man-power were made up by the issue, when and where necessary, of a special Press Warrant, valid only for "Seamen, Seafaring Men, and Persons whose Occupations and Callings are to work in Vessels and Boats upon Rivers." This was a rough and ready form of Selective Service, rendered necessary by the fact that there was no possibility of sending round polite call-up notices. The bureaucracy to do it did not exist, and anyway no one knew how many men were employed in these various pursuits, far less their names and addresses, and all efforts made by authority to discover them proved abortive. The Englishman of that time was not docketed from the cradle to the grave, indeed the government was not even aware of his existence. But when the Navy wanted trained seamen and gunners—plough-boys were not in demand—it knew where to get them. They were in the merchant ships, enduring conditions just as harsh as in the vessels of His Majesty, but being well paid for it and able to maintain some sort of family life. Therefore, the Press Gang operated mainly at sea, taking men off inward bound merchantmen. By 1778, however, the situation was so desperate that the net was legally flung wide, to include all able-bodied men, not specifically sailors.

The law of action and reaction at once came into play; the Merchant Navy set up a parallel organisation to the Press

Gangs, to induce seamen to desert the King's Service in favour of theirs, offering rum and still higher pay, as well as forged documents to enable them to cover their tracks. The Merchant recruiting agents were known as "crimps." A famous pair at Greenock were listed as "M'Kirdy & M'Lean, petty-fogging writers" (i.e., forgers). An equally famous pair —Henry Nathan and Sampson Samuel—eventually suffered the Navy's retribution; they were themselves "Prest"—and immediately "shipped foreign". The counterfeit documents did not always bear close scrutiny. Cato Martin, a seaman of the *Dolly* East Indiaman, produced for inspection by the Press Gang a "Protection" certificate which described him as having red hair and blue eyes. Unfortunately for him, he was a coal-black Negro—and soon found himself in a British warship. After the War of American Independence a false certificate of American citizenship was highly valued, being difficult to expose—owing to the similarity of the spoken variety of the two languages at that time. But many of the seamen could not read even their own certificates, as in the case of one Englishman who showed an American pass, according to which he had left America on the 29th of May and arrived at the American Consulate in London on the 6th of June, having apparently crossed the Atlantic in eight days. It would have been something of a record for the time.

Sometimes a homeward-bound crew of a merchant ship, seeing the Gang tender coming out to board them when, after many years abroad, they were within sight of England again, would offer savage resistance. The Portsmouth tender *Princess Augusta* was once fired upon by the crew of the merchantman *Britannia,* who had decided that they were not going to be pressed by such a "pimping vessel". Under a blaze of covering musketry fire, the Gang boarded and fought hand to hand with the seamen, who resisted with harpoons and the cook's spit. Three were killed, and buried at the low tide mark "without St. Helens", the anchorage near Spithead.

For those who were pressed, life in a warship was not so very different from the harsh conditions of a merchant ship; the full impact of naval discipline was felt only by those civilian volunteers who, usually in wartime, joined the Navy to defend their country or from a sense of adventure, and whose idea of life at sea was gained from Admiralty propaganda.

Apart from the severity of the punishments, the method of instilling the routine of automatic obedience to orders—vital to any Service—will be instantly recognisable to millions who served in the Second World War; it was applied noticeably where the raw material—the men—was very varied in quality, and where the jobs they had to be trained to do together were of a comparatively simple nature. It was based, to begin with at any rate, on fear; on driving; on instant submission on the one hand, and curt command on the other; on the utter inconsequence of the men, and the glittering importance of the officers. And it worked. It was this rigid system under which William Bligh was trained, and in which he implicitly believed; when he got his own first naval command —the *Bounty*—he continued to apply the method.

Its justification was—and is—the existence, in any group of men arbitrarily picked and thrown together, of a tough, brutal element who will take advantage of any leniency. There certainly were such men among the crew of the *Bounty*. But gearing discipline to the lowest element produced the inevitable result of degrading the best. It was no accident that the "port" area of Portsmouth was "nightly the scene of Bacchanalian orgies, tumults, and conflicts that must have given sober-minded strangers the impression that they had fallen upon an earthly pandemonium." Nearly half the taverns of Portsmouth were crammed into a tiny area around the small merchant ship harbour of the Camber, known from the aroma of its mudflats as "Spice Island." There were fairly sober establishments, such as the "Star and Garter", which catered for the lieutenant strata of a highly rigid society. The very junior officers frequented the "Blue Posts"; at the "Blue Anchor" in Broad Street the mutiny at Spithead was to be planned by seamen from the *Mars.* A stake and iron ring in the street outside was for the baiting of bulls on Shrove Tuesday; it was not so long since the practice of covering rats in turpentine and then setting fire to them had been current in Broad Street. It had been put down because of the danger of a fire being caused in the magazines of the harbour defences. Cock-fighting was a favourite sport in the taverns, attended frequently by officers—often quite senior officers—who dressed as seamen for the purpose.

Executions were normally carried out from warships moored in full view of Portsmouth "Point", the black, struggling figures being run up to the yardarms; three members of the *Bounty's* crew were to die there in that fashion. There, too, aboard the *Monarch* in 1757 Admiral Byng had been shot to death, "to encourage the rest." Savage as these sentences seem, they were comparatively civilised. It was only five years since, in 1782, David Tyrie, a convicted traitor, had been hanged, drawn, and quartered in public. As the screaming man was ritually cut to pieces, a mob of Portsmouth citizens surged around for a better view, eventually breaking the cordon and literally fighting each other for the dismembered portions of his body, and cutting it into still smaller pieces. A Gosport innkeeper got the head and put it on display, to increase custom.

Such were the riff-raff who, because of the Press Gangs, were likely to find themselves serving His Majesty at short notice; with such specimens the officers of His Majesty's ships had to contend. Naturally, there was a school of thought which favoured flogging as a punishment, and which was opposed to giving them the vote.

Spice Island was strategically placed to receive boats from both the harbour and Spithead, and also to send out boats to the ships lying in the anchorage. "After having moored our ship," wrote a seaman, "swarms of boats came round us; some were what are generally termed bum-boats, but are really nothing but floating chandler's shops; and a great many of them were freighted with cargoes of ladies, a sight that was truly gratifying." They were carefully selected by the boatman before leaving the beach, he says. "Old Charon surveys them from stem to stern, with the eyes of a bargaining Jew; and carefully culls out the best looking, and the most dashingly dressed; and it often happens that he refuses to take some of them, observing, (very politely) and usually with some vulgar oath; to one, that she is too old; to another, that she is too ugly; and that he shall not be able to sell them; for it has often been known that the officer in command has so far forgot himself as to order the waterman to push off—that he should not bring such a cargo of d—d ugly devils on board, and that he would not allow any of his men to have them. Of all the human race, these poor young creatures are the most pitiable; the ill-usage and the degradation they are driven to submit to, are indescribable; but from habit they become callous, indifferent as to the delicacy of speech and behaviour, and so totally lost to all sense of shame, that they seem to retain no quality which properly belongs to woman, but the shape and the name."

For the crew of the *Bounty*, there were to be equivalent scenes in the South Seas, but the Pacific seemed far away as the ship rolled and tossed at Spithead in the bitter winter weather. For Lieutenant Bligh it was a time of frustration. He had had his ship at Spithead, ready to sail, on November 4. He watched nearly three weeks of favourable winds pass by, merely waiting on the Admiralty for sailing orders; when they eventually arrived, the good weather had broken and the wind was foul. Ordinarily, it might not have mattered, but he was ordered to pass into the Pacific by way of Cape Horn, which was likely to prove impossible so late in the year. He applied for, and got, discretionary powers to take the alternative route around the Cape of Good Hope, if it should prove necessary. While waiting for them, he grumbled bitterly, "If there is any punishment that ought to be inflicted on a set of men for neglect, I am sure it ought on the Admiralty . . . This has made my task a very arduous one—to get round Cape Horn at the time I shall be there. Yet I must do it if the ship will stand it at all or I suppose my character will be at stake. Had Lord Howe sweetened this difficult task by giving me promotion . . ."

Bligh, an expert on South Sea navigation, was very bitter at still remaining a lieutenant when in charge of so important an enterprise; he started on his momentous voyage an angry man, feeling himself slighted, but sure that if he could make the venture a success, then the foundations of an important naval career were assured for him. He was determined that it should succeed; that by no fault of his, no oversight or neglect of forethought, should this great chance be forfeited.

But he had already made one mistake, a tiny one. While still at Deptford, he had had two cheeses from the ship's stores taken to his own house; as he was purser as well as captain, and entitled to make a small profit to recompense him for the additional trouble, he may have taken them in lieu, and thought nothing of it. His mind was set on more important matters. He was well aware that the particular path he had been treading for some years now—of which the *Bounty*'s voyage could be a culmination—led towards the coveted academic honours of the Royal Society. It would be extremely useful to make a distinctive niche for himself in the Navy, while still so junior in rank. This rather humourless man cannot have guessed just how closely his name was to be linked in future with the "Breadfruit" of the South Seas.

At length the weather changed, the *Bounty* prepared to sail. A sense of anticipation and adventure pervaded the ship now, mixed with half-stifled regret. "It is not the happiest moment of a sailor's life when he has to part with his Nancy," wrote a British sailor who experienced many such partings. "But grieving's a folly, and, upon these occasions they generally throw grief and temporary affection over the taffrail, as commodities they do not take to sea with them. Some men, being full of frolic and fun, would very politely offer a few onions to those ladies who could not contrive to get up a cry without their aid; this creates a little merriment, and is generally taken in good part by the ladies, whose hearts are not very sensible of the tender passions. But there were a few who felt the separation with concern; here and there one man would appear chap-fallen; another would heave a sigh; whilst others might be seen to drop a tear, not being able to calculate when they might meet again."

As the men walked the capstan bars round, and the dripping anchor ropes came inboard, the half-blind Irish fiddler, Michael Byrn, struck up the traditional air, "Drops of Brandy", and the men hummed the words to themselves.

And Johhny shall have a new bonnet
And Johhny shall go to the fair,
And Johhny shall have a blue ribbon
To tie up his bonny brown hair.
And why should I not love Johhny
And why should not Johhny love me,
And why should I not love Johhny
As well as another bodie.

To the tune of the old country dance the *Bounty* got under weigh. Soon they were passing close inshore to the Isle of Wight, the green English fields nearer than they would be again for many years. A pilot came aboard to take them out through the Needles Channel, and soon they were in the open sea, the towering chalk cliffs of the western coast of the Isle of Wight fading behind them. The voyage had begun. It was the 23rd of December, 1787. Tomorrow was Christmas Eve.

2
"I'll Give You a Damn'd Good Flogging!"

THE crew of the *Bounty* were mainly Anglo-Saxons; their commanding officer was not. Although William Bligh was born in Plymouth in 1754, the Blighs were Cornish; that is to say, Celts. Cornwall, and indeed virtually the entire western section of the British Isles, is the repository of the defeated, the site of last-ditch resistance to waves of invaders coming from the south-east and east. A line drawn down the centre of England and Scotland on a north-south axis would be a real dividing line, however blurred its edges, representing different peoples, a border between two contrasted sets of values. Between the passionate Celt and the stolid Anglo-Saxon there is little understanding or sympathy, but rather an instinctive antagonism. It is not enough to understand William Bligh; it is necessary to grasp how he appeared to the majority of his crew; there is a double judgement involved.

Some of his most characteristic traits were an almost comical exaggeration of what an Englishman finds most distasteful in certain foreigners. He talked with his hands. He was light-tongued, too, volleying abuse to let off steam, and making threats which he never meant to carry out. He had a fierce professional pride in himself and the naval service, but quite failed to see how damaging his conduct could be to the pride of others. Where the welfare of his crew and their efficiency were one and the same thing, he was thoughtful and far-sighted. Yet he habitually was unable to prevent himself from striking at the roots of discipline in his own ship by foully abusing the competence of his officers in the hearing of the men, and of shaking his fists threateningly in their faces, as if he was about to hit them. In his long and distinguished career he was three times to do this too often.

On two occasions he came up against Scotsmen who resented the injury to pride more than most. One of them was only a junior officer, when Bligh was a Post-Captain; the junior officer had his captain court-martialled and reprimanded. The other was a civilian, when Bligh was a Colonial Governor; he had Bligh arrested, deposed, and packed off home to England. But once—the first time—there was tragedy; on his first command of a warship, there was a mutiny, not only among the crew but among the officers as well; many lives were lost or ruined because of William Bligh. And yet he was not a harsh man; not a hard character; not a tyrant. If he had been, perhaps there would have been no mutiny on the *Bounty*. A hard man, if he had kept his temper, would probably have been respected. But that was the one thing Bligh could never do; he committed the unforgivable—trying to control other men without first being able to control himself. What he earned was hatred mixed with contempt. The two essential ingredients of mutiny.

There were exceptions. Some men understood him. Jewell, a boatswain who served him later, stated that Bligh had frequently called him a villain, a scoundrel, had said "if he had him in a dark corner he would do his business for him"; and had once forcibly shaken him and torn his shirt. Then he added, "Captain Bligh is very hot, and hasty, but I believe the words are no sooner escaped him, than his passion ends." That was in 1804; but that the Captain Bligh of 1804 was the same in essence as the Lieutenant Bligh of the *Bounty* is shown by an almost identical statement from a letter written by Ledward, the assistant surgeon, as the ship lay at Spithead in 1787: "The captain, though a passionate man, is, I believe, a goodhearted man and has behaved very handsomely to me."

A good deal of understanding, not to say forbearance, must however have been required from men whom Bligh manhandled or abused. "Passion", was the word frequently applied to his manner; or as we would say, temperamental, unstable, excitable. He called a gunner "a damn'd long pelt of a Bitch". There is a distinction between coarse language and a personal insult; Bligh had the knack of unforgivable insult, and probably did not realize it.

Where this habit became not merely unforgivable but positively unwise was when the words were addressed to an officer in front of subordinates from whom he was supposed to exact respect and obedience. Again in 1804, there is an example. While an officer, Lieutenant Frazier, was correcting a wardroom steward for playing cards, Bligh came bursting out of his cabin, demanding to know why Frazier was talking so loudly. While the steward looked on, Frazier replied: "I beg your pardon, sir, I am not. I am answerable for the occurencies of my watch."

Perhaps there was a hint of cheek in Frazier's reply. Anyway, it was enough to set Bligh off, losing all control. He shook his fist in the lieutenant's face, shouting "What, sir, you damn'd rascal, you damn'd scoundrel, never was a man troubled with such a set of blackguards as I am. Take care, sir, I am looking out for you." The steward whom Frazier had been reprimanding doubtless enjoyed every moment of it; nor was he the only lower deck witness present—the story of the public humiliation of an officer must have been all over the ship in a very short time. It was, as Frazier complained, "unofficerlike conduct" on the part of Bligh who, if he felt aggrieved, should have had Frazier into his cabin for a private chat. As the incident occurred in home waters, the indignant officer had his remedy immediately at hand; he complained officially, and in consequence Bligh was reprimanded and "admonished to be in future more circumspect and correct in his language." For the officers and men of the *Bounty,* thousands of miles from home, there was to be no such swift remedy available.

But, as yet, there was no hint of trouble. On the contrary, the upper strata who ran the ship were virtually a Bligh family party, a clique consisting largely of personal friends of Bligh, of the Bligh family, or of his wife's family, the Bethams. The ship itself had been family property until purchased by the Admiralty, as her former name, *Bethia,* indicates; she had been owned by Bligh's uncle, who had been partly instrumental in getting Bligh appointed to command her. The other influence was Sir Joseph Banks, of the Royal Society, who had become aware of Bligh as a result of his part in Cook's third voyage—Bligh had made the charts to illustrate the book of the voyage, published in 1784 (and was drawing royalties on its sale). Banks visited the *Bounty* while she was still at Deptford, fitting out, and thought Bligh would make a good protégé in the business of South Sea exploration. "He is become my pupil by accident," wrote Banks. "I will make him a botanist by choice." The botanist appointed to the ship, David Nelson, was also chosen by Sir Joseph, as was his assistant, William Brown.

On the surface, then, at the start of the voyage, mutiny would have seemed a most unlikely event. There were strong unifying factors at work. Bligh even had time for a little family life. His wife and children came down to Portsmouth to see him off, taking lodgings in Cumberland Street, a few minutes walk from the dockyard. Even when the *Bounty* was under orders to sail immediately, and was merely waiting for a favourable wind, Bligh managed to slip ashore for a final visit to his family. The captain's absence from his ship at that time was not known even to Sir Joseph Banks, and indeed was something of an escapade, but, wrote Bligh on the day he sailed, "Lord Hood winked at my absence, as he did not imagine a change of wind any more than myself." In the same letter he wrote, "My little ship is in the best of order and my men and officers all good and feel happy under my directions."

That was probably true. The crew had been given two months' pay in advance on November 28 and had been busy spending it; floating shops of all kinds had congregated about the *Bounty*. A ship at Spithead on pay day looked like "Donny Brook fair, or a borough election afloat." It was impossible to keep discipline, and the officers usually made themselves scarce, for fear of being insulted by some drunken harlot; indeed, one enraged hussy once climbed a mast and from that vantage point waved her petticoats at the flagship. It was not only among the men that there were "hard cases" or confirmed toughs.

The crew of the *Bounty,* when she sailed, numbered forty-six in all; but during the time she was waiting to sail thirty-two men had deserted and been placed on the ship's "Run" list. There was nothing very unusual in this. As Mr. Temple Luttrell, M.P. for Milborne Port, had remarked in the House of Commons ten years before, during a debate on the manning of the Navy: "A multitude of pressed seamen have been drowned by attempting to swim ashore from their ships, or have been shot by the sentinels while they endeavoured to escape under cover of darkness; being driven to frenzy and despair for want even of a shadow of hope that they might one day or other be entitled to a legal discharge. . . ." The most discontented men had, therefore, already discharged themselves and, as far as is known, there were no pressed men among the crew of the *Bounty;* thus another factor which might have led to indiscipline and mutiny had been removed.

After Bligh, the most senior member of the crew was John Fryer, the master. He was an officer, but did not hold the King's Commission; his job was the navigation of the *Bounty*. He came from Wells, in Norfolk, and Bligh was very pleased with his capabilities, reporting: "The master is a very good man, and gives me every satisfaction." Although Fryer, with years of naval service behind him, was quite incapable of mutiny, Bligh soon turned him into an enemy, by tactlessly promoting a subordinate over his head.

This subordinate was Bligh's blue-eyed boy, the master's mate—Fletcher Christian. Christian, although born in Cumberland and educated at the same school as William Wordsworth the poet, came from a family long associated with the Isle of Man. Bligh's wife was of Manx extraction, and so too was Peter Heywood, one of the midshipmen. It looks as though Bligh had a temperamental affinity to people less stolid than the Anglo-Saxons. If so, it would be understandable. He knew Christian well, and Christian was his own selection for the post of master's mate; that is to say, he personally selected the man who was to be the chief mutineer.

Fletcher Christian was aged twenty-four at this time, while Bligh was thirty-three; both were educated men, but Bligh was much the more experienced seaman. Christian's brother, Edward, was a barrister-at-law and later a professor at Cambridge, a man of influence who was subsequently able to do Bligh a great deal of damage. Fletcher had made several voyages under Bligh when, between the wars, the latter had obtained employment in merchant ships; what he knew of navigation was due to Bligh. Indeed, the trouble Bligh took with him aroused jealousy in others. Edward Lamb, chief mate of Bligh's previous ship, the merchantman *Britannia,* was later to help Bligh by denigrating Christian: "When we got to sea and I saw your partiality for the young man, I gave him every advice and information in my power, though he went about every point of duty with a degree of indifference that to me was truly unpleasant; but you were blind to his faults and had him to dine and sup every other day in the cabin, and treated him like a brother in giving him every information."

The opinion that Christian was inefficient may be taken

with a pinch of salt; but that the unfortunate Fryer must have been disturbed when Bligh promoted the young man over his head, is plain. Christian himself was grateful to Bligh and, although he admitted to his brother Edward that Bligh was a difficult man to deal with, being "very passionate", he did not take the outbursts too seriously.

In appearance Christian "had a bright, pleasing countenance and tall commanding figure, well adapted to those feats of strength and agility which he so frequently exhibited on the passage to Otaheite." Bligh afterwards described him sourly as "strong made and rather bowlegged; subject to violent perspirations and particularly in his hands so that he soils anything he handles; fair complexion, light brown hair, very much tatowed; speaks with the Isle of Man accent." He had a romantic attraction for the ladies, which was reciprocated; the disgruntled Edward Lamb grumbled that he was "one of the most foolish young men I ever knew in regard to the sex."

But he did take the *Bounty* from Bligh, and ruled the mutineers, who included all the hard cases in the ship, with a firmer, because less erratic, hand than his former captain. Whereas Bligh had to work at the art of command, being no leader, Christian had it naturally. He told his brother Edward, after a voyage in the *Eurydice* under a Captain Courtenay, that "it was very easy to make one's self beloved and respected on board a ship. One had only to be always ready to obey one's superior officers, and to be kind to the common men, unless there was occasion for severity, and if you are severe when there is just occasion they will not like you the worse for it." Although Christian was to bring suffering and death to many of the crew of the *Bounty,* none of them except Bligh ever said a word against him; whereas the men who were to owe their lives to Bligh's forethought and professional ability had neither liking nor respect for their officially appointed captain.

The other Manxman on board was Peter Heywood, a midshipman, fifteen years old. His family and the family of Mrs. Bligh were friends, and Bligh himself knew them well. His father-in-law had asked him to take Heywood on the voyage, stating: "He is an ingenious young lad and has always been a favourite of mine and indeed everybody here." He seems to have been a decent boy, rather high-spirited and perhaps not very responsible; Bligh was later to try to get him hanged.

Altogether, four of the five midshipmen were previously known to Bligh. George Stewart's father had a house at Stromness, in the Orkneys, and had got to know Bligh when the latter was serving with Captain Cook and their ship put in to Stromness for shelter. He was twenty-one when he joined the *Bounty,* a thin, dark-haired, black-eyed, narrow-chested young man, but a good seaman. Thomas Hayward and John Hallet were both friends of the Blighs and the Bethams; Ann Hallet was a very close friend in particular of Mrs. Bligh. These two were the official midshipmen of the *Bounty;* doubtless, they thought themselves a cut above the rest who were supernumerary. The list of midshipmen is rounded out by Edward Young, believed to have been a nephew of Sir George Young; Bligh describes him as of "dark complexion and rather a bad look—has lost several of his fore teeth, and those that remain are all rotten". He was half West Indian, born on St Kitts.

Laurence Lebogue, the sailmaker, and John Norton, one of the quartermasters, had been with Bligh in the merchant ship *Britannia;* William Peckover, the gunner—a warrant officer—had served with Cook, so Bligh knew him, too. Of those in whose appointment he had had no hand, Bligh took exception to one only, Thomas Huggan, the surgeon. "His indolence and corpulency render him rather unfit for the voyage. I wish I may get him to change," wrote Bligh. He failed and, as a reserve surgeon, the Thomas Ledward who thought Bligh "a passionate man", but also "good hearted".

was signed on at the last moment. "The Navy board," wrote Ledward, "has not allowed her a Surgeon's Mate; but the Captain was unwilling to trust the lives of 45 men so far from home with only one Medical person on board. I therefore do the duty of a Surgeon's mate, though only entered as an able Sailor."

And so the *Bounty* sailed down the Channel at the start of her momentous voyage, down Channel and into history forever, her captain priding himself on having a "happy ship". Two days out of port, the crew were happy enough, tucking into a Christmas dinner of beef and plum pudding, and fortified against the weather by a more than usually generous allowance of rum. But the next day, there was a bitter, rising wind from the east which shrieked through the masts and yards; the little ship went rolling on before it, her bows pitching heavily and spray sweeping over the decks. Steadily, the wind increased to a full gale, the foaming crests of the grey seas riding up under the stern; one great wave broke completely over the stern, stove it in, drenching the ship's biscuit stored there. The boats on the quarterdeck were also stove in, and men fought to prevent them being washed away completely. To save the hogsheads of beer lashed on deck was impossible, they were taken overboard by the fury of the seas. The spare yards and spars in the starboard mainchains broke free. Between deck the ship was a chaos of loose gear, sodden clothing, and vomit. Bligh was forced to put into a port for repair damage, and January 6, 1788, the *Bounty*—festooned with shirts, trousers, blankets, and hammocks, newly washed and hung out to dry in the African sun—sighted the high peak of Teneriffe, and came to anchor in Santa Cruz Roads.

We know that the town was "beautifully picturesque", from the journal of George Hamilton, who sailed that way several years after the mutiny, as surgeon in the frigate sent out in the wake of the *Bounty,* with orders to recapture her.

His narrative of life on board another small ship, making much the same voyage under much the same conditions, provides an invaluable comparison, showing what was normal and what was not. Bligh, who had learned his business under Captain Cook was, as might be expected, a stickler for cleanliness and health, as well as a believer in the new dietary recommendations which were beginning to defeat scurvy, the curse of many ships on long voyages. Hence his insistence on the washing of the clothing fouled by the storm and his pride in having laid in a stock of sauerkraut to provide the missing vitamins. But Mr. Cherry, purser of the pursuing frigate *Pandora*, had also provided "sour crout", as Surgeon Hamilton calls it. "A cask of this grand antiscorbutic was kept open for the crew to eat as much of as they pleased." And he adds, "I here beg the reader's indulgence for a small digression on the health of the seamen, as it is a subject of much national importance." Clearly, the doctrines of Cook were being widely applied. The *Pandora* took on board water and a variety of fruits at Teneriffe; so did the *Bounty*—and Bligh added a pair of drip stones for purifying the water after it had been long enough in the cask to contain a small cosmos of living organisms. Bligh believed in inspissated juice of wort, but made no innovations. Somebody concerned with the *Pandora* did, however—he believed in a good cup of tea. Surgeon Hamilton testified to "the uncommon good effects we experienced from supplying the sick and convalescent with tea and sugar; this being the first time it has ever been introduced into His Majesty's service. It has crept into universal use; but will be sought with more avidity by those whose whole aliment consists chiefly of animal food, and that always salt, and often of the worst kind. It is an established fact that a pint of tea will satiate thirst more than a quart of water. Quartermasters, and real good Seamen has ever been observed to be regular in cooking their little pot of tea or coffee, and in America seamen going long voyages, always make it an article in their agreement to be supplied with tea and sugar."

Bligh wrote in a self-satisfied manner to his benefactor, Duncan Campbell, while the *Bounty* was still at Teneriffe, "I have the happiness to tell you my little ship does wonderfully well; my men are all well and cheerful and behave very well." But this was not true; he had had trouble with the men about the rations, and obviously he was worried about his accounting for the ship's stores, as he goes on to say, "Having much to think of and little or no assistance my mind is pretty well employed, and as my pursing depends on much circumspection and being ignorant in it with a worthless clerk, I have some embarassment, but as I trust nothing to anyone and keep my accounts clear, if I fail in rules of office I do not doubt of getting the better of it."

The letter is what we shall come to recognize as typical Bligh. First, a delicate compliment to the influential owners of the ship, coupled with a vote of thanks to himself for managing her so well. "I have her now the completest ship that ever swam, and she really looks like one fit to encounter difficulties, and is look'd at as such, knowing our voyage." After the complete line-shoot there follows something slightly shady —the broad hint that, due to no fault of Bligh's (naturally), there is all too much room for error in his accounting for the rations issued. It was as if he were taking pains to cover his tracks in advance. In case of future complaint, the letter would be valuable, ready-made evidence; in short, a "cover story" for any pecadillo. Most typical is the slight, in this connection, on the professional competence of those under him. The "worthless clerk" was John Samuel, a London Jew; very able at his job, he was the only man of the entire crew who was faithful to his captain to the end, and the only man of whom, at the end, Bligh had a good word to say. But here, it was in Bligh's interest to brand him as incompetent, and he did so. And finally, Bligh slips in a line about the men being "all well and cheerful and behave very well." Bligh always maintained (officially) that he had a "happy ship," right up to the moment when his crew came for him with bayonets and muskets; it was not true, and he knew it was not true. Indeed, a hint of the actual state of affairs is there, in the letter, where Bligh says he has had "some embarassment" about his accounts. That, at any rate, was true.

But we would never have known the details of his "embarassment" had it not been for James Morrison, the boatswain's mate. He was an educated man of thirty, slender, with long black hair and a rather sallow complexion; one of his arms was scarred from a wound made by a musket ball. From Bligh's account in the *Bounty's* log, it is apparent only that he used the gale to "write off" some of the stores, including ship's biscuit (known then in the Navy as "bread"). The January 3rd entry reads: "Condemned on survey 2109 lbs. of bread and one cask cheese, 150 lbs. nett, wash'd to pieces in the late gale of the 27th." But this was not the whole truth.

"The cheese was got up to air," noted Morrison, "when on opening the casks two cheeses were missed by Mr. Bligh who declared that they were stolen."

Hillbrant, the cooper, was indignant. He was a stocky, fair-haired German, from Hanover—the home of King George—and he spoke English badly. In a thick guttural accent, he protested to Bligh that the cask had been opened before, when the *Bounty* was still lying in the Thames. Mr. Samuel, the clerk, had given him the order and the cheeses had been taken to Mr. Bligh's own house in London.

Bligh in a rage was an amazing sight. "He has a great deal of action with his hands," dryly testified an officer who knew him well, "as if he were going to knock any person down."

He went into action now, screaming at everyone—officers and crew alike—that they must all know who had stolen the cheeses. Their allowance of cheese would be stopped until the deficiency had been made good, he shouted. Then he turned to the unfortunate cooper and screamed out that he would give him "a damn'd good flogging" if he opened his mouth again about the cheeses.

He stalked away, leaving behind him a dumbfounded group of officers and men; and all of them made to feel like naughty schoolboys. There was a savage murmuring among the crew, and a tossing to-and-fro of evidence. John Williams, an able seaman, angrily clinched the matter. He had, he said, himself carried the cheeses to Mr. Bligh's house, together with a cask of vinegar and other items he couldn't remember; they had been taken in the ship's boat from Long Reach. There was no doubt of the facts. The question was: what could be done about it? In sullen fury, the crew decided to make a demonstration.

Cheese was served on banyan, or meatless, days, so when the next banyan day came round and Mr. Samuel the clerk served them out with butter, but no cheese, they refused to accept it. To do so, they told him, would be to admit, tacitly, that they acknowledged that the thief was among their number. They would admit no such thing; the thief was not in their mess.

On the following banyan day there was again no cheese; and again the men refused to accept the butter. Only when cheese was issued once more did they take the butter.

Bligh had conjured up a situation not unlike that depicted in the warning lines:

> When he stands like an ox in the furrow,
> With his sullen eyes set on your own,
> And mutters, "This isn't fair dealing"—
> My son, leave the Saxon alone!

It is doubtful if Bligh then—or ever—fully realized how deep was the resentment he was capable of arousing; but that he knew it existed, and was "fly" enough to take precautions, we do know. Why otherwise the reference to the efficient Samuel in his letter as a "worthless clerk." It was Samuel who had ordered Hillbrant to open the cask and to have the cheeses taken to Bligh's house. If ever there was an enquiry made, it would be useful to be able to blame a "worthless clerk" and the muddle he had caused in the accounts. And useful, too, to have proof that the *Bounty* was a "happy ship" at the time; hence, no doubt, the statement that the men (who, according to Bligh, had stolen the cheese) were "well and cheerful and behave very well."

It was probably unfortunate, in the circumstances, that the man most concerned, with Bligh, in the removal of the cheeses and in the subsequent attempt to pin the blame for the theft on the crew, was John Samuel. The fact that Samuel was a Jew had a significance, in naval ports, which it does not have now. There was business there for the poorer type of Jew, provided that he was sufficiently clever and not too scrupulous. The whore trade seems to have been mainly in the hands of Anglo-Saxons, but the floating chandlers shops with their cheap goods were largely Jewish run. This was a convenient and necessary service, providing also a cover for the smuggling ashore of dutiable goods by means of which the sailor made up his miserable pay. These Jews were also prepared to cash the sailor's pay cheques for them, at a considerable discount, and often to advance them money against the pay, with an even greater rake-off, because of the very real risk of their being bilked by the sailors. The actual villains of the piece were the Admiralty, with their absurdly complicated pay regulations, but it was the cheap-jack traders and small-time money lenders who came in for the full blast of the sailor's resentment. There is hardly a narrative of the time which does not refer, with irritation and contempt, to the "land sharks" of the ports. Samuel was not in fact that type of Jew at all; he was a very self-contained and courageous man; and what he did in the *Bounty* was at the direct orders of William Bligh. But, this early in the voyage, the direct association of a Cornishman and a Jew in a "fiddle" over the rations, followed by an unscrupulous attempt to foist the blame onto a lot of honest Englishmen, must have helped to set them all against Samuel as well as their captain; and once their stolid minds were set in that direction, it would have taken a very great deal to change them.

In retrospect, the affair of the stolen cheeses seems a small thing; but it was not. It marked the point when William Bligh lost the respect of his crew, the basis of real discipline.

3

"*I'll Make You Eat Grass!*"

THE *Bounty* left Teneriffe on January 10, 1788, and the self-satisfied Bligh took a momentous decision, for which he duly voted himself three cheers in the log. "I now ordered my people to be at three watches," he wrote, "and gave the charge of the third watch to a Mr. Fletcher Christian, one of the mates." Having made that fatal appointment, he went on to congratulate himself for his professional efficiency, in dividing the crew into three watches instead of two. "I have ever considered this among seamen as conducive to health, and not being jaded by keeping on deck every other four hours, it adds much to their content and chearfulness." Put like that, it sounds as if Bligh were the only one to promote the idea; but in the pursuing *Pandora* the same system was followed. "The dividing the people into three watches had a double good effect," wrote Surgeon Hamilton of the *Pandora*, "as it gave them longer time to sleep, and dry themselves before they turned in; and as most of our crew consisted of landsmen, the fewer people being on deck at a time, rendered it necessary to exert themselves more in learning their duty." It was not, as might be thought, a matter of humanity—Captain Edward Edwards of the *Pandora* was a savagely ruthless officer beside whom Bligh appears more as a fussy old woman than a grim tyrant. The fact is, that it was an officer's duty to keep his men fit and healthy and that the system of four hours on and four hours off was necessary only in emergency conditions, such as being in enemy waters in wartime.

Bligh was very conscious of his duty in this respect, and he filled out the log entry by adding, "Some time for relaxation and mirth is absolutely necessary, and I have considered it so much so that after 4 o'clock the evening is laid aside for their amusement and dancing. I had great difficulty before I left England to get a man to play the violin and I preferred at last to take one two-thirds blind than come without one." The blind fiddler was the little Irishman, Michael Byrn, aged twenty-eight. Bligh thought so highly of the value of his music in relieving the tedium and harshness of a long sea voyage, that when hands were ordered up to "dance and skylark" he made the sick join in, too, as Morrison noted in his journal. Perhaps Bligh really thought it would do them good.

As the *Bounty* sailed into the South Atlantic towards the Equator, conditions between decks became foul. On February 2, Bligh noted: "All this morning empl'd making points and drying wet cloaths and airing and cleaning below, for the air being very sultry and damp it is all I can do to keep the people's accommodation, clean and wholesome." Bligh's care for his "people" (as the crew were then called) was not, as has sometimes been claimed, exceptional; he used fires to air their quarters, but the captain of the *Pandora* actually had a ventilator installed for this purpose. The ambitious young lieutenant was technically competent and kept abreast of current practice, but no more can be claimed for him than that.

On February 16 another ship was sighted; it proved to be the whaler *British Queen,* which took aboard the *Bounty's* mail for England. One of the letters was from Bligh to Duncan Campbell. The lieutenant wrote: "We are all in good spirits and my little ship fit to go round a half score of worlds. My men all active good fellows, and what has given me much pleasure is that I have not yet been obliged to punish any one. My officers and young gentlemen are all tractable and well disposed, and we now understand each other so well that we shall remain so the whole voyage, unless I fall out with the Doctor, who I have trouble to prevent from being in bed 15 hours out of the twenty-four. My men are not badly off as they share in all but the poultry, and with much content and chearfulness, dancing always from 4 until eight at night. I am happy to hope I shall bring them all home well. Tom Ellison is a very good Boy and will do very well."

Ellison was a stocky little fellow of seventeen; almost Bligh's last sight of him, many months later, was when he was waving a bayonet in Bligh's face; nor did he do very well. On the contrary, he died at the yardarm of the *Brunswick* in Portsmouth harbour for his part in the mutiny of the *Bounty*.

That at any rate Bligh could not have guessed, but the rest of the letter seems merely an attempt to impress an influential shipowner with his own capabilities as a captain; for it is a truism that there are no bad sailors—only bad officers—and that bad officers have also to punish more often than good officers.

On March 2 Bligh promoted his favourite, Fletcher Christian, as acting Lieutenant making him the highest ranking man in the ship after himself. The senior warrant officer—the master, John Fryer, an older and much more experienced man—now ranked third. Bligh himself had been appointed a master by Cook and eventually obtained a commission (as opposed to a warrant) as Lieutenant. A commission is signed by the reigning monarch and is much more prestigious than a warrant; but the master, as senior warrant officer, was a most important man. Nowadays, in a merchant ship (as opposed to a warship) there is no difference between the Captain and the Master; they are the same person. In a warship, the highest ranking executive officer is called the Captain, even if, like Bligh, his rank is lieutenant.

The apparent confusion in the navy of Bligh's time goes back centuries to the beginnings of sea warfare, originally waged by what were in fact armed merchantmen. In time of war the experienced shipmaster was still in charge of the sailing of the vessel, but he was joined by a military man, trained to war, who directed fighting tactics and commanded the soldiers aboard. There was also a more subtle distinction in English ships, that of class. The military man, the "Captain", was part of a warrior caste who regarded themselves as superior to the common people and had a divine right to govern. Not everyone saw it their way.

By Bligh's time the master was still the navigator and controlled the ship's sailing; but there were six grades. When he joined the *Bounty*, Fryer had qualified as a master of the 3rd rate; he subsequently earned golden opinions from such famous captains as Thomas Fremantle and Thomas Foley, was recommended by Vice-Admiral Sir Hyde Parker, and retired, at the top of his profession, as a master of the 1st rate. It has been argued (Du Rietz, 1979) that the profession was a dead end, with transfer to commissioned rank difficult, and that therefore Fryer cannot have regarded the promotion by young Bligh of a still younger man to acting lieutenant as a blow to his professional pride. But it must have been, even if Fryer accepted the inevitability of the better born being given command. Certainly, Fryer was too professional to express any resentment openly or to let it affect his work—he would do his duty. But would he do more than his duty, if that was required? And there was to come a time when Bligh's future was to hang on whether or not Fryer would risk his life for him.

As the *Bounty* neared the Equator, there was a series of explosions from the men about their food. Bligh had already warned them that they were in for a long voyage, whose length was uncertain, and that therefore he was reducing the bread ration by one-third. This was accepted without a murmur, as necessary impositions usually are. The revolt—for it was nothing less—came when the pumpkins which Bligh had taken on board at Teneriffe to replace stores lost in the gale, began to go bad. To use them up as quickly as possible, they were immediately issued instead of bread. Then, wrote Morrison: "The people being desirous to know at what rate the exchange was to be, enquired of Mr. Samuel, who informed them that they were to have one pound of pumpion in lieu of two pounds of bread." That did it, for this wasn't "fair dealing."

"They refused, and on Mr. Bligh's being informed of it, he came up in a violent passion, and calld all hands, telling Mr. Samuel to call the first man of every mess and let him see who would dare refuse it or anything else he should order to be served, saying, 'You dam'd infernal scoundrels, I'll make you eat grass or any thing you can catch before I have done with you!' "

The revolt collapsed. "Everyone took the pumpion as calld, officers not excepted, who tho it was in their eyes an imposition said nothing against it, tho it was plain to be seen that they felt it more severely than the men, who having yet a good private stock of potatoes which they had laid in at Spithead did not immediately feel the effects of such a reduction."

Although his language was tactless and intemperate, Bligh might even have been right here; but it made little difference, the men were already set against him. He quelled the revolt, certainly, but at the cost of making them even more stubborn. They merely bided their time, waiting for a better excuse. The pattern of contest between captain and crew, introduced at Teneriffe, had now become established. That Bligh met the occasion with immoderate language but moderate treatment, is also clear. So far, his bark was infinitely worse than his bite. Probably he was overanxious in husbanding the food; certainly, he was no sadist. His log entry for February 10, the day after the *Bounty* crossed the Line, shows it:

"This afternoon those who had never crossed the Line before underwent the usual ceremony except ducking, which I never would allow for of all customs it is the most brutal and inhuman. Twenty seven men and officers were therefore tarred and shaved with a piece of iron hoop, and the officers to pay two bottles of rum and the men one, which I promised to answer for, and gave every one a half pint of wine as soon as the business was over, and dancing began."

As the pumpkin issue was so small, the crew soon used up their private stocks of potatoes in supplementing it; at the same time, says Morrison, "the beef and pork began to appear very light, and as there had never yet been any weighed when opend, it was supposed that the casks ran short of their weight." They thought Bligh and Samuel were cheating them. This time, they took their complaint to Mr. Fryer, hoping he would put in a word for them. Obviously, they had given up hope of getting justice, or even a hearing, from Lieutenant Bligh. But, if they had hoped to get a hearing in this manner, they were mistaken. Bligh took it as a slight to his authority, and acted accordingly; he ordered all the men to assemble aft, and then, according to Morrison, "informed them that evry thing relative to the provisions was transacted by his orders, and it was, therefore, needless to make any complaint for they would get no redress, as *he* was the fittest judge of what was right or wrong. He added, that he would flog the first man severely who should dare attempt to make any complaint in future and dismissed them with severe threats."

The result was what might be expected. "The seamen seeing that no redress could be had before the end of the voyage, determined to bear it with patience, and neither murmur'd or complaind afterwards." Bligh would not have been Bligh if he had not taken that sullen silence for proof that he was right, and had his crew in hand again. But, more ominous still, was the different attitude adopted by the officers; they "were not so easy satisfied and made frequent murmurings among themselves about the smallness of their allowance." Bligh's happy little family party was coming to pieces around him. Particularly galling to the officers was to see "with regret all the prime pieces taken out for the cabbin table"—i.e., for Bligh's own use. But, perversely, the fact that the officers were as badly off as the crew "helped to make the men reconciled to their part, seeing that it was not level'd at them alone, but that all shared a like fate." In the short run, that was favourable for Bligh; in the long run, it was to be disastrous. Apart from Mr. Samuel, he had no friend in the ship.

In his own eyes, Bligh was not being tyrannical; he was merely being careful to husband the stores and at the same time showing his unruly crew that he meant to stand no nonsense, reasserting the authority he had lost early in the voyage. The men saw it differently. It was not the quality of the food they had complained about, but the amount. It was not frivolousness, or fastidiousness, that was the centre of their grievance, but simply that they were not getting enough to eat. They were hungry. And they were angry, and the officers angrier still, because they suspected Bligh was helping himself to the best food out of each cask, for himself and Mr. Samuel. But as soon as they saw there was nothing to be done about it—as soon, in fact, as they had lost all faith in Bligh—their complaints abruptly ceased. This was characteristic; the British grumble only when they believe they can achieve something. Now, they would have to use other means; wait until the end of the voyage, and put in a claim against Bligh, as purser, to make up in cash the deficiencies in their rations, which was a legal method of redress.

Bligh later got hold of Morrison's narrative and wrote an answer to the allegations contained in it. Naturally, he denied nearly everything—not once in his career did he admit a mistake or a lapse from professional conduct. When criticised, he invariably produced an absurd outburst of praise for himself and his methods. He did so in this case, ending his denial with: "So happily did every person with him (Bligh) feel themselves, that letters from the people and warrant officers were particular in remarking how happy they were under Captain Bligh's command—His treatment of them was such that songs were made on him extolling his kindness."

This, to coin a phrase, is pure Bligh.

His method can best be studied by examining the two sides of the case: the parallel entries made by Bligh, in his official log, and Morrison, in his unofficial account. On March 23, Bligh recorded: "In the morning I killed a sheep and served it to the ship's company, which gave them a pleasant meal." But on March 23, Morrison wrote: "One of the sheep *dying*, this morning Lieut. Bligh order'd it to be issued in lieu of the day's allowance of pork and pease, declaring that it would make a delicious meal and that it weighed upwards of fifty pounds; it was devided and most part of it thrown overboard, and some dried shark supplyd its place for Sundays dinner, for it was no other than skin and bone."

Bligh made a number of entries to the effect that "wheat and barly were now boiled every morning in lieu of burgoo" (porridge). Certainly they were, for Morrison referred to them also: "The quantity was so small, that it was no uncommon thing for four men in a mess to draw lots for the breakfast, and to devide their bread by the well known method of 'who shall have this,' nor was the officers a hair behind the men at it."

This method, although no longer used to raffle off essential rations, is still sometimes invoked as a means of impartial division. Even the "banyan day" has endured, slightly altered, into modern times; a banyan in the Navy now being, instead of an official meatless day on board, a boat expedition for the purpose of angling, spear-fishing, skin-diving, or just plain lazing on a beach. As the fish caught are usually cooked and eaten on the spot, the original meaning of the word is fairly well preserved. A number of other terms—such as calling a sentimental person a "soft toad"—have likewise endured, showing a surprising continuity and high-lighting the fact that the men who sailed with Bligh were mostly not so very different from ourselves. The detailed proof of it can be read in the many naval memoirs of the time. The machinery of a sailing ship was less complicated, and there were more seamen employed in hard manual work and fewer technical specialists, but the men themselves were much the same.

The one great difference—passed over almost unremarked in the journals being kept in the *Bounty,* because it was so normal—was the severity of the punishments inflicted at sea. Bligh had already entered in his logbook, on March 11, "Until this afternoon I had hopes I could have performed the voyage without punishment to any one, but I found it necessary to punish Matthew Quintal with 2 dozen lashes for insolence and contempt." Later, much later, he added the words "to the Master." Morrison, complaining bitterly throughout this period of the inadequacy of the food rations, did not think this incident worth even half a line in his diary. He did not mention it at all. Quintal was a short stocky youth of 21, a seaman who later became one of the mutineers. Probably he was one of the "hard cases" aboard. Such men represented a practical problem for their captain. On the one hand, as Bligh recognized, to inflict severe punishment was a confession of failure on the part of the officer; it proved that he had been unable to dominate his crew by force of personality alone. On the other hand, very few men have this capacity to the degree required, and, in practice, the officer could either punish severely or not at all.

In a modern Service the officer has two deadly weapons at hand—the stoppage of leave and of pay; in effect, he can inflict a hell of boredom on the offender for a considerable period. This is particularly effective with the hard case—or the merely high-spirited man—who lives for his gambling and booze. But the naval officer of the eighteenth century had no such power; the men were paid only at long intervals and they rarely got leave. In addition, the drink ration on board was a good deal more liberal than it is today. If the man was to be punished, but at the same time kept available for duty, the lash—but not too much of it—was the only weapon available. At the same time, even a dozen lashes was a severe punishment; it might not break the man's back, but it could break his spirit—to be tied up to a grating and publicly flogged until he screamed in agony in front of his messmates, was likely to shatter a man's self-respect, turn him into a sullen brute. There was a deterrent effect on the others, of course, provided that only a few were flogged; but if such punishment was handed out right-left-and-centre, each man would begin to wonder when his turn would come for this humiliating treatment; there would be a savage tension in the ship. And Bligh, once he had broken his resolution not to punish and had tasted blood, went on; in his long-drawn-out contest with his crew, he flogged again and again. Quintal was to be merely one of many.

The one man whom young Bligh could not discipline was the old surgeon, Thomas Huggan. A doctor was in a privileged position. To Huggan, Bligh was an insolent young puppy; and against Huggan, Bligh was helpless. He could only rage in his log, "I now find my doctor to be a drunken sot, he is constantly in liquor, having a private stock by him, which, I have assured him, shall be taken away, if he does not desist from making himself such a beast." But Huggan was a dying man, and probably he knew it. The threats of the ambitious, pushing young officer had no power to move him; and doubtless this additional failure in his long contest for command rankled with Bligh. He never did part Huggan from his liquor. All he did was to add another enemy to the long list of enemies he already had in the ship.

However, as the *Bounty* rolled on towards Cape Horn, a greater disciplinarian than Bligh took over. From March 24 to April 22, they had no sight of land. Gale after gale came howling down upon the little, struggling ship. A vicious cross-sea, with wind and tide contending, raised enormous breakers round her. With mere rags of sail set, the *Bounty* climbed up the mountainous waves, and went sliding down the other side. She seemed walled in by the sea she was so desperately fighting. Squalls of sleet and snow swept across the decks, chilling to the bone the men exposed to the elements; water washed across the planking and poured down the gangways. The sullen clank of the pumps formed an hourly background to the shrill moaning of the wind through the distended rigging. The sails became coarse and heavy with snow, so that it was an impossible agony to set them when required. In order to get his navigational observations, Bligh had to be lashed in place with a rope. A cloud of soaring blue petrels followed the labouring ship, and once two seals were sighted, impervious to the threat of thundering water which imperilled the frail wooden vessel.

The cold and damp of the living conditions in their wildly tossing home, together with the dull ache of hunger bred by inadequate rations and hard, often desperate, labour on deck, led to sickness. "Violent sickness and vomiting and severe head ach", were the symptoms recorded by Bligh in the log. Some were doubtless seasickness cases but others, equally obviously, were not. There was fighting over the division of the rations, according to Morrison. "This scanty allowance caused frequent broils in the galley, and in the present bad weather was often like to be attended with bad consequences and in one of these disputes the cook, Thos Hall, got two of his ribbs broke & at another time Churchill (Charles Churchill, the Ship's Corporal) got his hand scalded and it became at last necessary to have the Mrs mate of the watch to superintend the division of it." Bligh duly reported the fractured rib case, but put it down entirely to "the violent motion of the ship," omitting to mention the primary cause. From his own point of view, he was justified in keeping the rations short. With weather like this, which he had anticipated even before he left Spithead, there was no telling the duration of the voyage. Apart from the food, he did everything he could to ease the hardships of his men, keeping a fire going below in order to dry their clothes. By April 12 he had taken the extreme step of giving up his own cabin every night to the more unfortunate members of the crew whose own sleeping quarters were now more or less permanently awash. This was Bligh at his best, the ruthlessly efficient officer driving his frail sailing machine into the tempest of tortured waters round the Horn, and seeing to the comfort of his men before he saw to his own. In a brute struggle with the fury of the weather, or when hammering out hull-to-hull broadsides with an enemy in battle, Bligh was a captain to follow. The *Bounty,* for all the battering she took off the Horn, never lost a spar, or a fragment of canvas. But she was not gaining in her attempt to force her way into the Pacific. "The greater part of the time," wrote Bligh, "we were doing little better than drifting before the wind."

In this severe test, his crew did not fail him, and Bligh was moved to try a disciplinary measure new for him—praise. "As the people began to fall sick," wrote Morrison, "the duty became heavier on the Well, but was still carried on with alacrity and spirit, and the behaviour of the Seamen, in this trying situation, was such as Merrited the entire approbation of the Officers and Mr. Bligh's thanks in a Publick speech." Conscious that he might be held professionally to blame for not carrying out his orders to the letter, Bligh held on doggedly until the fourth week of April, when he was "hourly losing ground." If he put about, the winds which now kept him out of the Pacific would blow him into it around the tip of Africa. "Having maturely considered all circumstances," he wrote, "I determined to bear away for the Cape of Good Hope; and at five o'clock on the evening of the 22nd, the wind then blowing strong at W, I ordered the helm to be put a weather, to the great joy of every person on board. Our sick list at this time had increased to eight, mostly with rheumatic complaints: in other respects the people were in good health, though exceedingly jaded." In this hour of apparent defeat, Bligh's stock stood at its highest. Momentarily, he had the chance of making permanent the unity which the gales of the Horn had imposed on captain, officers, and crew.

Day after day the *Bounty* rode on across the South Atlantic, with hardly an incident worth recording. On May 22, Table Mountain rose up above the horizon, and the *Bounty's* guns began to thunder out a salute, returned gun for gun by the Dutch fort at Cape Town. Hardly had the powder smoke drifted away on the wind, than John Williams, a Guernsey seaman who spoke French, was spreadeagled on the gratings, with the lash tearing at his naked back. "Punished John Williams with 6 lashes for neglect of duty in heaving the lead," noted Bligh in his log. Possibly the punishment was justified—it could have been—but it seems curious that there were no such signs of slackness during the entire month spent off the Horn. Perhaps the gale absorbed all Bligh's energies, and left him no time for petty fault-finding; certainly, his outbursts of fury coincided only with periods of calm. In any event, he had another sullen foe aboard—for Williams, like Quintal, was to join the mutineers.

During the time spent re-fitting at Cape Town, Bligh wrote a characteristic letter to Duncan Campbell, his former employer, the influential ship and estate owner. It was a disarming attempt to show, by implication, how good an officer was William Bligh, addressed to a man who might mention it casually in places where it could count most.

Bligh was old for a lieutenant, he yearned for his captaincy. "I am satisfactorily repaid for all my trouble," he wrote, "by bringing them all here without a single complaint." He mentions casually, "a Dutch ship came in to-day, having buryed 30 men . . . this is a credit I hope will be given to me as my ship is not roomly or of size to be comfortable. Indeed had I not been conversant with these matters I believe poor fellows they would scarce ever have got here." The ability of William Bligh was not going to pass unnoticed, if William Bligh could help it. Then, without a blush, he wrote, "Upon the whole no people could live better. I fed them with hot breakfasts of ground wheat and sugar" (there had been broken ribs over the distribution of that). "Portable soup and krout equal to cabbage made a valuable meal," he went on. "Pease also mixed with the two former articles was equal to the greatest dainty and I supplyed half their allowance of salt meat by giving them flour and raisins in lieu." And, meeting perhaps a suspicion before it had even been thought, he added, "I assure you I have not acted the purser with them for profits was trifling to me while I had so much at stake. I do not repine, but if the cruel inattention of the Admiralty had not detained me I should certainly have made my passage round the land."

Had he been "acting the purser"? There is a clue to Bligh's character in mercenary matters in another letter to Campbell, also written from Cape Town. "My transactions here have enabled me to realize a little cash, for which I beg leave to transmit to you an indorsed Bill to you by Christoffel Brand, Esqr. on the Victualling Board for 1.236 Rix Dollars which will be paid immediately as it becomes due." Clearly, William Bligh was not averse to chasing a fast buck. He appeared to be uncommonly adroit at it, too.

4

"*The Paradise of the World*"

ON JULY 29, after thirty-eight days at Cape Town, the *Bounty* steered out of False Bay and set course for the southern coast of Australia, Bligh intending to pass into the Pacific by way of Tasmania and New Zealand. He did not take a direct route because, as he wrote, "I shall endeavour to pursue a new track by which means it will be of use to future navigators and the voyage may very properly so far be said to be of discoveries." Bligh may very properly be said to have been half-blind throughout the voyage; he was pre-occupied, as his log shows, with making a separate name for himself as an explorer and navigator of partly unknown seas; to be, not merely a pupil of Cook, which he was, but an equal. He set himself to the task with painstaking thoroughness. He recorded every seal, each type of seabird, even the presence of floating weed. He checked the position of every island sighted with the published maps and charts, and was, in many cases, delighted to find that they were inaccurate. He was constantly on the lookout for a rock, a reef, or an island which was *not* on any chart, so that he could log an actual discovery and not merely a correction—which might, after all, be incorrect. Dating from his voyage with Cook, Bligh was always correcting other people, scribbling his own acid comments over their published books and maps; the observations of the great explorer himself were not immune from the righteous venom of his subordinate. Often, he scribbled in pencil, sometimes in ink, occasionally—when particularly infuriated—in red ink. These savage entries, in which he criticises everything and everybody, especially his superiors, are revealing—because they were private. They were the real Bligh, bursting with jealous fury, always right, and always surrounded by fools, as it appeared to him. No wonder he was passed over for promotion—and how that must have inflamed his already vengeful sense of self-righteousness! This voyage of the *Bounty* was to be his answer to them all—the proof of what William Bligh could do, when he held the power of command. This obsession with the necessity for producing obvious and outstanding success blinded him to the reality of the situation—that what he had to do, he could not do alone. His officers and crew were instruments—"children," he called them—of his will. He had to keep them healthy, if they were to be of use to him, in the same way that he had to keep the ship seaworthy, if it was to complete the voyage, but he drove men and ship hard, unable to realize that those under him, having no reason to, were unlikely to share his own savagely determined enthusiasm. There would be no honour and glory for them, only for their commander. Had Bligh been able to communicate some of his own feelings to his ship's company, and so to become their leader instead of their taskmaster, he might indeed have secured the triumph he sought. Instead, he was merely to provide himself with the opportunity of scoring yet more manuscripts—particularly Morrison's—with red ink; and, eventually, to provide Charles Laughton, Trevor Howard and others with a number of excellent acting opportunities. His reactions to these portrayals would have been worth recording.

The tyrant—he was not, of course, a tyrant in his own eyes—did not have matters all his own way. In his warrant officers, protected by their rank against such obvious punishments as flogging, and very conscious of it, as of the dignity that went with the rank, he met a sullen obstacle. Because the warrant officers had the same social background as the men they controlled, and were in close contact with them, that dignity—based on age, experience and seniority—had to be firmly buttressed all the time. That was particularly so in the case of a small ship, where men lived cheek-by-jowl; less so in a monster ship-of-the-line, which was more like a floating barracks, with marines, and bands, and pipeclay. Bligh, in his impatience, chose to undermine the position of these key men in the disciplinary plan of the ship.

On August 21, the *Bounty* anchored in Adventure Bay, part of what was then known as Van Diemen's Land, and is today Tasmania. Bligh intended to refill the water casks and to try to net fish to supplement the rations. The catch, he reported, consisted of "a few flounders and others like a soul but not so good, with some flat-headed fish called by a fisherman on board, foxes, but of little value as to size or taste, the whole not amounting to twenty."

Bligh soon began to find fault with the working parties. The first man he picked on was William Purcell, the carpenter, a warrant officer responsible for the condition of the ship's structure who was ashore in charge of a wood-collecting party. "On my expressing my disapprobation of his conduct with respect to orders he had received from me concerning the mode of working with the wooding Party," wrote Bligh, "he behaved in a most insolent and reprehensible manner. I therefore, ordered him on board, there to assist in the general duty of the ship, as I could not bear the loss of an able working and healthy man; otherwise I should have committed him to close confinement." Bligh apparently could not leave an experienced technician alone to get on with the job in his own way: Purcell may have implied as much. According to Morrison, Bligh's interference was not limited to Purcell; he also "found fault with the innatention of the rest, which produced continual disputes evry one endeavouring to thwart the others in their duty." As an exercise in man-management, Bligh's methods were producing lamentable results. Within the week, he again had trouble with Purcell.

The incensed carpenter stood on his rights, carefully defined as they were. The working parties being small, and Bligh in a hurry, he told Fryer, the master, to see to it that all the officers took their share of hard manual labour. The warrant officers were not supposed to do this, partly to preserve their status and partly because they were often elderly men. When told by Fryer to assist in hoisting heavy water casks into the hold, Purcell flatly refused. Bligh was ashore at the time, but when told of what had occurred, he sought out Purcell in a fury. Bligh reported bitterly in the log, "but my directions and presence had as little effect" (as had Fryer's). "He said he would do anything in his line, but as to that duty he could not comply with." The raging Bligh was not to be beaten by the stubborn man. He put on a high-handed act, ordered legal depositions to be made and signed by witnesses; then ordered, what was illegal, to deprive Purcell of all rations until he consented to do the manual labour. If any man would dare to assist the carpenter by giving him food, Bligh threatened him "a severe punishment." That Bligh found this latter threat necessary was an ominous indication of the mood of his crew. Any ascendency he had gained over them in the storm-battles round the Horn, had gone. But he had his little victory—the humiliated warrant officer went to work alongside the men to whom he, in his turn, was expected to give orders which would be obeyed unquestioningly.

On September 19, as the *Bounty* was passing into the Pacific south of New Zealand, "a cluster of small rocky islands" was sighted. Delightedly, Bligh wrote, "Captain Cook's track, in 1773, was near this spot, but he did not see the islands . . . I have named them after the ship, the Bounty

Isles," he announced proudly. Lieutenant Bligh was on the map. But on October 9, when well into the Pacific, trouble again exploded.

In the morning, he pitched in to the surgeon, Thomas Huggan. The truth of the matter will never be known—we have Bligh's account only. According to Bligh, one of the seamen, James Valentine, who had been ill, was reported to him as being delirious and dying. Bligh says he was shocked, because the doctor had said he was getting better. "I therefore, sent for the Surgeon and was perhaps severe for his remissness. However, all I could get out of him was that he intended to have told me of it last night, but as I was not alone (having according to custom the officer of the Watch to sup with me,) he did not think it proper; that he must now inform me that he had not many hours to live." This, said Bligh, gave him "very unfavourable ideas" about the capacity of the doctor.

Within a few hours he was involved in a most public row with his second in command, the master, John Fryer. Mr. Samuel, Bligh's clerk, came hurrying to his captain with a troublesome matter concerning the accounts. The monthly account books, together with the boatswain's and carpenter's expense books, duly signed by Bligh as being a true statement, had to be counter-signed by the master. When Samuel had shown Fryer the accounts, Fryer had refused his signature. Then he had agreed to sign, according to Bligh's statement, if Bligh would sign a certificate that Fryer "had been doing nothing amiss during his time on board." In short, if there was a "fiddle" in the accounts, Fryer wanted to be absolved of all blame. "As I did not approve of him doing his duty conditionally," wrote Bligh, "I sent for him and told him the consequence, when he left me abruptly saying he would not sign the books upon such conditions." Morrison's journal amplifies Bligh's account of what happened then.

"All hands were called aft, and the Articles of War read,

and some part of the Printed Instructions; after which the books and papers were produced with a pen and ink, and Mr. Bligh said 'Now Sir, sign them books.' The master took the pen and said 'I sign in obedience to your orders, but this may be cancelld hereafter,' the books being signed, the people were dismiss'd to return to their duty."

For the log, Bligh concluded his account by adding, "This troublesome Man saw his error, and before the whole ship's Company signed the Books and here again I forgave him."

Again, Bligh had won a little victory, publicly brow-beating his second in command, but this time with less effect on the crew; some of them were puzzled as to what it had all been about. The general drift of the affair can, however, be gauged by recalling the matter of the stolen cheese (taken to Bligh's home), Bligh's keen speculating at Cape Town, and the final summing up, given many years later in an Army report on Bligh to the Secretary of State, which characterised his failings as two-fold: "his longing to gratify his insatiably tyrannic disposition and to advance his pecuniary interest."

The result of that day's work, as noted by Morrison, was: "Mr. Bligh and his mess mates, the Master and Surgeon, fell out, and separated, each taking his part of the stock, & retiring to live in their own cabbins, after which they had several disputes & seldom spoke but on duty; and even then with much apparent reserve."

There was some sickness in the ship, the men complaining of rheumatic pains, the surgeon diagnosing it as scurvy, and Bligh—probably wrathful that such a thing should happen in his ship, despite the precautions he had learned from Captain Cook—brushing it aside as "nothing more than the prickly heat." One of these sick men was ordered by Bligh to take part in the dancing which, thought Bligh, was "conducive to their health." The man, William Brown, said he was too ill to dance, so Bligh ordered his grog to be stopped "with a promise of further punishment on a second refusal."

The surgeon, Huggan, was also on the sick list, which

Bligh entered in the log as being entirely due to drink. On October 22, he noted: "This day I sent for the Surgeon and in the most friendly manner requested him to leave off drinking, but he seemed not sensible of any thing I said to him and it had little effect. The Surgeon kept his bed all this day and always drunk, without eating an ounce of food. If it is ever necessary this should be publickly known, I may be blamed for not searching his Cabbin and taking all liquor from him." Bligh's brisk threat, made earlier in the voyage, to do exactly that, had apparently not been carried out. How much truth there was in Bligh's accusations we do not know; all that we do know is that the surgeon was a dying man, with only six weeks more to live.

On October 25, at half-past seven in the morning, the crew of the *Bounty* saw a distant speck, their first South Sea Island. It was Maitea, not far from Tahiti. In the afternoon, they ran close along its northern coast; and began to make out houses, coconut groves, and, finally, a group of natives waving to them from beyond the surf. Like a great white seabird, the European ship floated past paradise. Bligh had seen it all before, but for many of his crew the islands of the Pacific were a magical legend, now rising up before them in reality. More than 26,000 miles of ocean, according to Bligh's reckoning, had passed under their keel since leaving the bleak, wintry anchorage of Spithead. Now, golden beaches and blue, translucent coral seas confronted them, sparkling in a heart-warming sunshine. The first British ship to see them, the *Dolphin,* coming under attack by canoes off Tahiti, had opened up with her cannon, filling the crystal clear water with the brownish smoke of blood. Subsequently, a Lieutenant Furneaux had landed a party without opposition, raised a standard, and taken possession of the island in the name of King George III. Neither side had taken lasting offence at the nature of their introduction—indeed, the power of the Europeans and the bravery and skill of the natives, being thus proven, resulted in a mutual respect. However, for a sailor, the lure of the islands was not merely the classic longing of man for sun, sand, and sea, but for the golden girls without whom it would be a harsh waste; and the women of these islands were reputedly as lovely as they were compliant. To Bligh, this was no legend, bawdily exaggerated in the mess-decks; it was fact. While he had spent half of his time impatiently feuding with his officers and crew, with the other part of his mind he had been pre-occupied, planning for this moment. At all costs, he must succeed in obtaining the breadfruit—and that meant establishing and maintaining good relations with the natives. They, unlike his crew, were not under his orders. They must be conciliated, not browbeaten. And the crew of the *Bounty*, rough-necks as some of them were, must not be allowed to give them cause for offence. He began to issue a series of long-thought out instructions.

The first was to the surgeon, Thomas Huggan. Short-arm inspection for everyone on board. Or, as Bligh put it, "As I have some reason to suppose the Otaheiteans have not been visited by any ships since Captain Cook, I hope they may have found means together with their natural way of living, to have eradicated the Venereal disease. To prove this and free us from any ill founded Suppositions, that we might renew the Complaint, I have directed the Surgeon to examine very particularly every Man and Officer and report to me his proceedings. This was accordingly done and he reported every person totally free from the Venereal complaint." They were not long to remain so.

Next was a list of written orders for the guidance of his crew, six points being made.

"1. At the Society, or Friendly Islands, no person whatever is to intimate that Captain Cook was killed by Indians; or that he is dead."

"2. No person is ever to speak, or give the least hint, that we have come on purpose to get the bread-fruit plant, until I have made my plan known to the chiefs." Bligh knew that the chiefs would offer him gifts to take back to the King, and among these, he hoped, would be the bread-fruit; he would therefore be able to accept it as a gift, instead of something to be bargained for.

"3. Every person is to study to gain the good will and esteem of the natives; to treat them with all kindness; and not to take from them by violent means, any thing they may have stolen; and no one is ever to fire, but in defence of his life." Bligh knew, again from his experience with Cook, that anything which was not actually tied down was likely to "walk." To the lower orders among the natives, a European ship was a treasure house of wealth, the bulk of the manufactured articles being beyond the power of their economy to produce—and therefore unique. His fourth point placed the blame for any losses squarely on the shoulders of his men.

"4. Every person employed on service is to take care that no arms, or impliments of any kind under their charge, are stolen; the value of such thing, being lost shall be charged against their wages." All very proper, but the vigilance required would have to be almost superhuman.

"5. No man is to embezzle, or offer to sale, directly, or indirectly, any part of the King's stores, of what nature soever." Again, very proper; this is a temptation to which, occasionally, the English still fall prey. The sixth, and last, point was more restrictive.

"6. A proper person or persons will be appointed to regulate trade, and barter with the natives; and no officer or seaman, or other person belonging to the ship, is to trade for any kind of provisions, or curiosities; but if such officer or seaman wishes to purchase any particular thing, he is to apply to the provider to do it for him. By this means a regular market will be carried on, and all disputes, which otherwise may happen with the natives, will be avoided."

This final point intended to avoid "all disputes" with the natives, led to serious trouble, because it meant, taken to extremes, as Bligh took it, that no native could give any gift to a particular friend on board the ship without having it confiscated by Bligh. His instructions were logical, one can see his point; but behind them was Bligh's unstated, driving purpose to succeed in his mission, to which everything else was to be utterly subordinated. A wiser captain would not have interfered so meanly in private matters; but, to Bligh, his crew were not human beings, with lives and desires of their own, but merely instruments of his will, placed implacably under his orders. The disputes, when they came, appeared therefore unbelievably petty. They were anything but that in fact; they were the sullen, obstinate resistance of the Anglo-Saxon to being "badgered about" unreasonbly.

On October 26, these orders having been issued, the *Bounty* sailed slowly into Matavai Bay, Tahiti, and with happy, friendly natives already swarming on board, let go her anchor in thirteen fathoms. Bligh had arrived in what he himself described as "the Paradise of the World."

The palm-fringed shore of Tahiti was backed by conical, volcanic-looking mountains, from which cool rivers ran down to the sea. The temperature was so warm that houses in the European sense were unnecessary—the homes of the natives being like a rather exotic sort of cattle shed, with a thatched roof, supported on posts, curving down towards the ground, but not reaching it. The floors were strewn with hay, covered in turn by mats. In that climate, they were airy, pleasant places, and those of the chiefs were very large; larger still was the community house of the village, which might exceed two hundred feet in length. Around the houses was the welcome shade of the woods, which also provided food without much work—breadfruit, coconuts, bananas. Hogs provided meat and there were fish in plenty in the clear depths of the blue sea. As Captain Cook remarked, when he first saw Tahiti, here there was no necessity that "man should eat his bread in the sweat of his brow." And here, Surgeon Hamilton was to observe in due course, "human nature appears in more amiable colours, and the soul of man, free from the gripping hand of want, acts with a liberality and bounty that does honour to his God. The earth without tillage produces both food and clothing, the trees loaded with the richest of fruit, the carpet of nature spread with the most odoriferous flowers, and the fair ones ever willing to fill your arms with love." Truly, a sailor's paradise, after the rough living and raw male discipline of a King's ship.

Every contemporary account we have—and there are many—speaks with admiration of the people of the islands, but duly noting that there were two classes. "The shape of the face is comely; the cheekbones are not high, neither are the eyes hollow, nor the brow prominent; the nose is a little, but not much, flattened; but their eyes, and more particularly those of the women, are full of expression, sometimes sparkling with fire, and sometimes melting with softness; their teeth also are, almost without exception, most beautifully even and white, and their breath perfectly without taint. In their motions there is at once vigour as well as ease; their walk is graceful, their deportment liberal, and their behaviour to strangers and to each other affable and courteous. In their dispositions they appear to be brave, open, and candid, without suspicion or treachery, cruelty or revenge."

We know also how their English visitors appeared to the natives. According to Hamilton, "The English are allowed by the rest of the world, and I believe with some degree of justice, to be generous, charitable people; but the Otaheitans could not help bestowing the most contemptuous word in their language upon us, which is, Peery, Peery, or Stingy."

Bligh, although not strictly speaking English, acted true to type. He at once got down to his business. The omens were favourable. Within a few hours of anchoring out in the bay, a man arrived on board with a picture of Captain Cook (whom the natives called Toote). This painting was exhibited as a token of friendship and, the frame having been broken, they asked for it to be repaired. Bligh was surprised to learn that they knew of Cook's death—but not that he had died at the hands of natives. The news had been obtained from a British ship which had called some months before. Next morning, Bligh worked the *Bounty* to within a few hundred years of the shore, anchoring in seven fathoms. Later that day the local chief came out in one of the ship's boats. "After introducing his wife to me," wrote Bligh, "we joined noses, the customary manner of saluting, and, to perpetuate our friendship, he desired we should exchange names. I was surprised to find that instead of Otoo, the name by which he formerly went, he was now called Tinah. He was a very large man, not less than six feet four inches in height and proportionately stout." Tinah was thirty-five; his wife, Iddeah, was about ten years younger, tall above the average, and with "a very animated and intelligent countenance." The chief presented Bligh with a large quantity of cloth, a large hog, and, significantly, some breadfruit. In return, Bligh took the royal party to his cabin and formally presented Tinah with some "hatchets, small adzes, files, gimblets, saws, looking glasses, red feathers, and two shirts." The ship was well-stocked with such goods, chosen for their value to natives living on an island which, unlike England, was not built on coal and iron. The presents were gratefully accepted, indeed they were rather too much of a success. "To Iddeah I gave earrings, necklaces, and beads; but she expressed a desire also for iron, and therefore I made the same assortment for her as I had for her husband. They appeared extremely satisfied; so that they determined to spend the day with me, and requested I would show them all over the ship. This, though I was not fond of doing, I indulged them in; and the consequence was, as I had apprehended, that they took a fancy to so many things, that they got from me nearly as much more as I had before given them. Afterwards, Tinah desired me to fire some of the great guns; this I likewise complied with, and, as the shot fell into the sea at a great distance, all the natives expressed their surprise by loud shouts and acclamations. When he left the ship, he requested I would keep for him all the presents I had given him, as he had not, at Matavai, a place sufficiently safe to secure them from being stolen. This is perhaps not so much a proof of his want of power, as of the estimation in which they hold European commodities, and which makes more than the common means of security requisite to prevent theft."

The pay-off came the next day, when Bligh was expected to return the call by visiting the chief. Bligh took care to have a number of presents transported with him, and to carry himself a large supply of beads; he was accompanied to Tinàh's house by a large crowd and, like a vote-soliciting politician, distributed the beads to the children, with, he wrote, "much drollery and good-humour." The public-relations act satisfactorily completed, Bligh and Tinah began to discuss the events which had occurred since Bligh's last visit. There had been some fighting on nearby islands, between rival tribes. Then, wrote Bligh, "Tinah, understanding from my conversation that I intended visiting some of the other islands in this neighbourhood, very earnestly desired I would not think of leaving Matavai. 'Here,' said he, 'you shall be supplied plentifully with every thing you want. All here are your friends, and friends of King George; if you go to the other islands, you will have every thing stolen from you!' I replied, that, on account of their goodwill, and from a desire to serve him and his country, King George had sent out those valuable presents to him: 'and will not you, Tinah, send something to King George in return?' 'Yes,' he said, 'I will send him any thing I have'; and then began to enumerate the different articles in his power, among which he mentioned the bread-fruit. This was the exact point to which I wished to bring the conversation; and, seizing an opportunity, which had every appearance of being undesigned and accidental, I told him the breadfruit trees were what King George would like; upon which he promised me a great many should be put on board, and seemed much delighted to find it so easily in his power to send any thing that would be well received by King George. I had now, instead of appearing to receive a favour, brought the chiefs to believe that I was doing them a kindness in carrying the plants, as a present from them to the Earee Rahie no Britannee."

Clearly, in one respect at least, Bligh had been a very good choice to command this mission. Within a matter of forty-eight hours, he had been completely successful. Immediately, he sent Fletcher Christian ashore with a party to erect a tent for the temporary reception of the breadfruit plants as they were collected, and the botanist, Nelson, with his assistant, Brown, were placed in charge. There was only one snag. The breadfruit was in flower, and could not be transplanted for some time. Further, Bligh's sailing orders directed him to return by Endeavour Straits, and the best season for that was some time ahead. It would be necessary—strictly on duty—for Bligh and his men to remain at Tahiti for nearly half a year. To be precise, they were all to have a paid holiday—for there was little work to do, except guard the ship—in a South Sea island paradise for what must have seemed almost an indefinite period. Endlessly golden days stretched before them, lazily in the warmth beside the brilliant blue of the Pacific.

An approximate replica of HM armed vessel *Bounty*, built for a Hollywood film. The real breadfruit carrier was a former merchant ship named the *Bethia*, with stumpy masts cut down to make her safer in bad weather – quite unlike the towering clipper-type canvas of the replica.

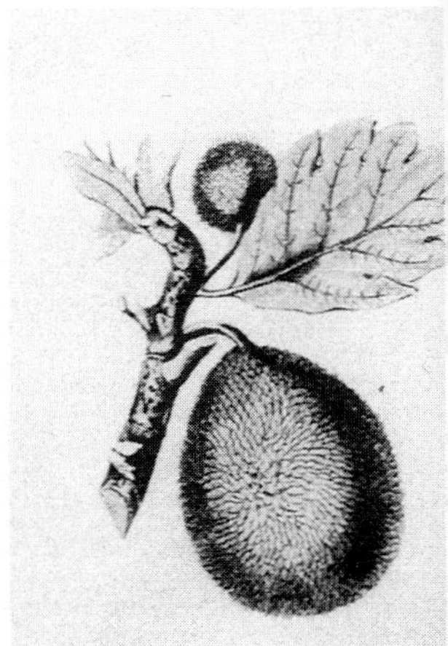

Bligh as Captain in 1803, from a painting by John Smart. *Photo: National Portrait Gallery, London*

The breadfruit plant. From an old print. *Photo: Alexander McKee*

A native dance in honour of European explorers in the Pacific. From an old print. *Photo: Alexander McKee*

5
Hell in Paradise

Bligh had not even completed his successful negotiations for the breadfruit plants, when he was able to write, "An intimacy between the natives, and our people, was already so general, that there was scarce a man in the ship who had not his *tyo* or friend." The *tyo* more-or-less adopted the officer or sailor, who was able to spend most of his off-duty time ashore in family surroundings, a practice known in modern times as "getting your feet under the table." This relief from the stark reminders of discipline aboard ship was at least as well appreciated as the admiring attitude of the ladies to their distinguished visitors from the other side of the world. More public entertainments were also organised by the Tahitians to amuse their guests; these often took the form of exhibition dances, known as *heivas*. Bligh was almost at once invited to one, which "lasted half an hour and consisted of wanton gestures and motions, such as have been described in the account of former voyages." Or, as a modern matelot put it, after watching the same sort of entertainment on another Pacific island, the dances were "highly interesting in a revolting sort of way."

Surgeon Hamilton was less inhibited when, a few years after Bligh, the ship's company of the *Pandora* was invited to a *heiva*. "The entertainment began by two men, who vie with each other in filthy lascivious attitudes, and frightful distortions of their mouths. These having performed their part, two ladies, pretty fancifully dressed, as described in Captain Cook's Voyages, were introduced after a little ceremony." (The girls were clothed only from the waist downwards, with lengths of clinging material which reached to their ankles). "Something resembling a turkey-cock's tail, and stuck on their rumps in a fan kind of fashion, about five feet in diameter, had a very good effect while the ladies kept their faces to us; but when in a bending attitude, they presented their rumps, to shew the wonderful agility of their loins; the effect is better conceived than described. After half an hours hard exercise, the dear creatures had remüé themselves into a perfect fureur, and the piece concluded by the ladies exposing that which is better felt than seen; and, in that state of nature, walked from the bottom of the theatre to the top where we were sitting on the grass, till they approached just by us, and then we complimented them in bowing, with all the honours of war." The dance was, of course, a love dance in which the Tahitians saw nothing unnatural or obscene, as even the coarse old doctor had to recognise. "These accomplishments are so much prized amongst them," he went on, "that girls came from the interior parts of the country, to the court residence, for improvement in the heiva; just as country gentlemen send their daughters to London boarding-schools."

Into the peace of the lazy Pacific islands fell at once the lash of Bligh's discipline. On November 3, a little over a week after anchoring in paradise, Bligh had one of his seamen triced up in front of all the natives crowded on deck; then the strokes of the lash began to cut into the man's bare back. "Several chiefs were on board at the time," he wrote, "and with their wives interceded for the man, but seeing it had no effect they retired and the women in general showed every degree of sympathy, which marked them to be the most humane and affectionate creatures in the World."

The man was known on board as Alexander Smith, but this name was false; his real name was John Adams. He was a Londoner, from Hackney, and an orphan, brought up in the poorhouse where the first thing he was taught was the Catechism. At this time he was 22 years old. His offence was that, while he was on duty, a native had stolen the gudgeon of the cutter's rudder. Water was no obstacle to the Tahitians, who could swim for miles for the sheer pleasure of it; they could dive, and stayed submerged, for lengths of time which appeared incredible to their European contemporaries, to whom the sport had yet to be introduced. This extraordinary skill, the implications of which were unsuspected by the *Bounty's* crew, was probably responsible for the ease with which, when they wanted to, they could arrive and depart unseen, particularly at night, taking with them some coveted piece of metalwork. Nothing, except the good will of the chiefs, or the constant dropping of explosive charges into the water, could have prevented it. A submersion time of between one and two-and-half minutes is not beyond the capacity of a fit young man on breath-holding alone, and in that time he might well be able to cover a distance in excess of fifty yards. If he merely wanted to disappear, motionless, with his head just under water, holding on to the hull to prevent himself from breaking surface, he could prolong his breath-holding to something in the nature of four minutes. In these conditions, a dishonest native virtually had the ship at his mercy. But Bligh put it down to laxity.

"Several petty thefts having been committed by the natives owing to the negligence and inattention of the Petty Officers and men, which has always more or less a tendency to alarm the chiefs, I was under the necessity this afternoon to punish Alexr Smith with 12 lashes," he wrote. And, he added, "I thought it would have a good effect to punish the boatkeeper in their presence." So John Adams, alias Alexander Smith, had his back cut to ribbons in order to impress the natives

A month later, early in December, Bligh again clashed with the obstinate warrant officer, Purcell. The carpenter had perhaps decided that the best way to deal with this arrogant young upstart was to "work to rule." Bligh, eager to conciliate the natives and maintain the essential friendly relationships, was entertaining the chiefs in his own cabin almost every day. When there was a request from some of the Tahitians that the resources of the European ship be used to cut a large stone into a grindstone fit for sharpening their hatchets, Bligh at once agreed, and gave the necessary orders to Purcell. The carpenter examined the stone, and then told Bligh he would not cut it. "It will spoil my chisel," he declared. "Though there is a law to take away my clothes, there is none to take away my tools." A carpenter cherished his tools as much as a conscientious modern Service driver looks after his maintenance kit, so Purcell's reluctance is understandable on ordinary grounds; but doubtless he also got a lot of satisfaction out of thwarting Bligh. He was within his rights, and he was also—as long as his equipment was in working order—a key man in the ship. Bligh blazed instantly with authority, and placed Purcell under close arrest. But next day, he released him. He would have to wait until he got Purcell to England, if he was to take real disciplinary measures. For their part, the crew also were waiting until they got back to England, to raise officially their past grievances against Bligh. And so the situation smouldered on, the latent discontent eased by the attractions of Tahiti. There was no thought of mutiny.

The pleasures of the land were not untainted, however. Previous visits by European ships had left their mark. A number of the men, and two of the officers—Fletcher Christian and the young midshipman Peter Heywood—realized with a sick horror that they had contacted V.D. The old surgeon, Huggan, was not of much use to them. By December 9, recorded Bligh, "Mr. Huggan had been a long time ill, the effects of intemperance and indolence. He had latterly scarce ever stirred out of his cabin, but was not apprehended to be in a dangerous state; nevertheless, this evening he appeared to be so much worse than usual, that it was thought necessary to remove him to some place where he could have more air; but to no effect, for he died in an hour afterwards." Bligh added, unfeelingly, "This unfortunate man drank very hard, and was so averse to exercise, that he never would be prevailed on to take half a dozen turns upon deck at a time, in the whole course of the voyage." The officially recorded aspersions on the dead man echo most curiously Bligh's remark on the death of his benefactor and teacher, Captain Cook, "his death was no more attended to in the course of a few days as if he never existed."

Huggan was buried ashore and Ledward, who had had medical training but had shipped aboard as an A.B., was appointed surgeon in his place. Ledward, like Nelson, the botanist, was a very quiet man whose duties did not in any way bring him into conflict with Bligh; but even he was to turn, in thought though not in deed, against his captain.

Soon afterwards, two more floggings took place—of Robert Lamb, the butcher, for "suffering his Cleaver to be stolen"; and of Matthew Thompson, seaman, for "insolence and disobedience of orders". Twelve lashes apiece. Five of the small crew had now been flogged. Yet here, in Tahiti, there was no need for flogging—confinement to the ship would have been punishment with "teeth" in it, particularly if the offender had been kept under close arrest while off-duty. Probably, the more effective alternative simply did not occur to Bligh; flogging was the traditional punishment, and he had no real understanding of, or sympathy with, his men. Also, it was quicker, all over and done with in a few minutes—as far as Bligh was concerned—which suited his impatient, variable temperament. But it was not over and done with in the minds of the men who suffered its bloody humiliation. And Bligh continued, even intensified, his conflict with the officers and crew as a whole; and came off worst, although he never suspected it.

Once again, it was a matter of rations, with Bligh conserving them in view of the long voyage ahead to deliver the breadfruit plants in the West Indies and probably making something for himself on the side; certainly interfering in the crew's private affairs. He had appointed William Peckover, the gunner, to take charge of the trade between the crew and the natives. The men had supplied themselves with hatchets, knives, files, gimlets, combs, looking glasses, and so on, from the floating shops at Spithead, knowing that these were what was most in demand in a primitive society. Then, as now, they had a very keen nose for the market, although this one was not exactly "black." But they were not after souvenirs of the South Seas. Their experiences with Bligh had put matters in proportion. As Morrison dryly observed, "No curiosity struck the seaman so forcibly as a roasted pig and some breadfruit." The trade was almost entirely in food. And it was at this that Bligh struck, to provision his ship from the private dealings of the men he had kept on short rations for so long. Unfair dealing indeed.

During December, wrote Morrison, "The market for hogs beginning now to slacken Mr. Bligh seized on all that come to the ship, big & small, dead or alive, taking them as his property, and serving them as the ship's allowance at one pound pr man pr day. He also seized on those belonging to the master, & kill'd them for the ship's use . . . and when the master spoke to him, telling him the hogs were his property, he told him that 'He, Mr. Bligh would convince him that evry thing was *his,* as soon as it was on board, that he would take nine tenths of any man's property and let him see who dared say anything to the contrary.' Those of the seamen were seized without ceremony, and it became a favour for a man to get a pound extra of his own hog."

Again, Bligh had taken steps which alienated the officers as well as the men; once more picking on the most senior of the officers, the master, John Fryer. What he was doing also alienated some of the natives, and, shortly, the officers, the men, and the natives were combining to cheat the unscrupulous Bligh. The contest was divided into two stages.

First, says Morrison, "The natives observing that the hogs were seized as soon as they came on board, and not knowing but they would be seized from them, as well as the people (the 'people' being the crew), became very shy of bringing a hog in sight of Lieut. Bligh either on board or on shore." They then tried the method of watching for Bligh to land and, when he was out of sight, taking out provisions to their friends in the *Bounty*. "But as Mr. Bligh observed this and saw that his diligence was like to be evaded he ordered a book to be kept in the bittacle wherein the mate of the watch was to insert the number of hogs or pigs with the weight of each that came into the ship."

After a little thought, the Tahitians came up with an answer to that, and stage two of the conflict—Bligh v. the Rest—began. "To remedy this," wrote Morrison, "the natives took another method which was cutting the pigs up and wrapping them in leaves and covering the meat with breadfruit in the baskets, and sometimes with peel'd cocoa nuts, by which means, as the bread was never seized, they were a match for all his industry; and he never suspected their artifice."

When Bligh was later shown Morrison's Journal, he scribbled answers to the various accusations; but, unlike his writings in the margins of the book concerning Cook's last voyage, they do not spurt forth fury and indignation. They are curiously lame. This case is a fair sample. He explains that he has already explained the circumstances to the Admiralty in his Log Books; he claims that the reason there were any hogs at all brought on board was "due to his influence with the natives of Otaheite"; contradicts this by going on to say that "every man's friends was bringing him roasted hogs every day, and when they brought live ones I could not permit them to run about the ship"; and that the purpose of the officer of the watch keeping a "hog book" in the binnacle was an economic survey—"Captain Bligh declares it was from no other motive but curiosity to ascertain the number of hogs received to show the supply the country gave them." A study of Bligh's muddled, lame replies on these occasions leaves the suspicion that it was not only hogs that were being cooked, but the *Bounty's* account books as well; that Bligh probably was "playing the purser". But, in this case, his crew outsmarted him, aided by the natives, whose motives were more of friendship to the seamen than of business.

On December 24 the breadfruit plants, the object of the voyage, were brought aboard the *Bounty;* there were 774 pots in all. So Christmas Eve was a day of hard work for the crew, and Christmas Day also, as Bligh had to shift his anchorage to a more secure one, and ran the ship aground in doing so. Afterwards, the pots were taken ashore opposite the new anchorage, until the full number should have been collected. The waters just off the nearby reefs were, for obvious reasons, a favourite fishing "mark" for the Tahitians, and Bligh was interested to observe their methods. They were two-fold—in the water, and out of it. The angling was done mainly at night, bright lights being used to dazzle the fish, the rods being made of bamboo. Bright, unbaited hooks were dropped into the water where, catching the light, they would gleam and attract the curiosity of the fish. The rest of the fishing was carried out, close to the reefs, by swimmers. Usually, they carried a handspear, but sometimes two men together would use a small net. From Bligh's account, they seem to have worked together—the swimmers close in and the anglers, with their torches lighting up the sea, further out. The swimmers must actually have dived on their prey, but Bligh, who noted the angling details carefully, gives only a blurred picture of the underwater side of these operations, which took place on almost every calm night, so that "the whole sea appears illuminated."

The New Year opened inauspiciously. On January 5, 1789, three men deserted from the *Bounty*. Two of them were seamen—William Muspratt and John Millward. The third was, of all people, Charles Churchill, the Ship's Corporal—the man responsible for policing the ship. Muspratt and Churchill were both aged 30—older than the average of the *Bounty's* crew. At 4 A.M., on the change-over of the watch, the ship's cutter was found to be gone. The matter was reported to Bligh, who mustered the men and held a roll call. Then the absence of the three men was discovered. Further investigation showed that eight muskets and ammunition pouches were missing also. "All owing to the Mate of the Watch being asleep on Deck," a furious Bligh scribbled in the log. The offender was a midshipman, Thomas Hayward, Bligh's own choice for the position because of the friendship between the Hayward family and Bligh's own relatives. Seen in that light, Bligh's log entry reads strangely: "Had the Mate of the Watch been awake no trouble of this kind would have happened—I have therefore disrated and turned him before the Mast. Such neglectful and worthless petty Officers I believe never was in a ship as are in this. No Orders for a few hours together are Obeyed by them, and their conduct in general is so bad, that no confidence or trust can be reposed in them—in short they have drove me to everything but Corporal punishment, and that must follow if they do not improve." Probably he would have done it instantly, had not four out of the five midshipmen been members of the "Bligh family party" with which he had stocked the ship. The warrant officers he could not flog—they were protected by their rank. Even Hayward was not flogged, but he was at once put in irons, and was to remain chained for no less than eleven weeks—an almost equally savage punishment.

In fact, Bligh was in a mood almost to rend his former friends. He ordered Fryer away in the large cutter to search for the smaller, stolen cutter. Fryer found it, being brought back to the *Bounty* by the natives, the deserters having landed. Meanwhile, Churchill's belongings had been searched. Among them had been found a piece of paper on which was written his own name and those of three of the men who were on duty ashore, under Fletcher Christian, guarding the breadfruit plants. That was enough for Bligh. Here was proof of further intended desertions—a plot! He went ashore in a blaze of fury, and according to Morrison, "informed Mr. Christian of the business calling the men and challenging them with being concerned with Churchill and intending to disert. They persisted in their innocence, and denyd it so firmly that he was inclined from circumstances to believe them and said no more about it." That was a bad mistake. If they had had no idea of desertion before, they certainly had it now.

Then Bligh cooled down, recollected Captain Cook's method of dealing with deserters, and sought out Tinah to apply it. Always work through the chiefs, never against them, or without their authority; make them responsible, as far as you can—that had been Cook's dictum. Bligh tried it, but found that the Tahitians showed understandable reluctance to attempt to capture men equipped with firearms. Anxiously, they asked: had the men pocket pistols, like Bligh? Bligh laughed, and assured them that they had only muskets. If the natives greeted the deserters as friends, and crowded round them, they could take and disarm them with ease and without danger. "I have no doubt they will bring the Deserters back," wrote Bligh, "but in case of failure I shall proceed to no extremities untill I have the Plants on board."

The midshipman Hayward had undoubtedly been at fault.

Morrison confirms Bligh's statement that the boy had been asleep while on watch. Things were getting slack in the *Bounty,* and Bligh's frequent rages and wholesale denunciations did nothing to improve matters. On January 17, he found more evidence of it. "This morning, the sail room being cleared to take the sails on shore to air. The new fore topsail and fore sail, main topmt stay sail and main stay sail were found very much mildewed and rotten in many places. If I had any officers to supercede the Master (John Fryer) and Boatswain (William Cole), or was capable of doing without them, considering them as common sea men, they should no longer occupy their respective stations." But none of the officers, having been chosen mostly by Bligh, were suitable. "Scarcely any neglect of duty can equal the criminality of this, for it appears that altho the sails have been taken out twice since I have been in the island, which I thought fully sufficient, and I had trusted to their reports, yet these new sails never were brought out or is it certain whether they have been out since we left England, yet notwithstanding as often as the sails were taken to air by my orders they were reported to me to be in good order." Yet John Fryer was to obtain glowing reports from the outstanding captains under whom he was later to serve, and to be promoted. It seems that the effect of William Bligh's personality was to bring out the worst in the men he commanded. And his uncontrolled rages had no effect whatever, but rather the reverse of what was intended, producing sullen hostility instead of a smartening of discipline.

At 5:30 P.M. on January 22, word was brought to Bligh that the three missing men were living in a village some miles up the coast. He immediately set off in one of the ship's boats and, in the failing light, made a difficult passage through the reefs on which a sea was breaking. Once ashore, he met Teppahoo, a local chief, from whom the message had originally come. This man told him that the deserters were living in a house near to his own. While Bligh went with the natives along the beach, the ship's boat followed just offshore—to have left it on the beach unattended would not have been wise. Bligh took none of his crew with him, but, at the head of a group of Tahitians, went straight to the house. As he approached, Churchill, Muspratt, and Millward emerged. They were unarmed, and told Bligh they wanted to give themselves up. As there was no safe landing for the boat at that point, he told a native to swim out to it and tell the men to take it back down the coast to the point where he had landed. And then the little party set off, the triumphant Bligh, and the three miserable men who knew that they had committed, this time, a really serious crime, and what the horrifying punishment must be. It was a very stormy evening. The wind roared through the coconut trees and the rain poured down solidly, as the little party, accompanied by the Tahitians, trudged along the slushy paths to the beach and the sea. That night, Bligh and two men from the boat slept in a hut ashore, guarding the deserters, while the rest of the men got what sleep they could under an awning in the boat.

Next morning the three men were taken out to the *Bounty*, and put in irons. Twenty-four hours later, the grim ceremonial of punishment took place. First, Bligh read out the Articles of War. He intended that this punishment was to be an example to everyone in the ship, officers and men alike. The deserters were to have their punishment in instalments —half the lashes now, and half in two week's time. Churchill was to have twenty-four lashes in all, Muspratt and Millward forty-eight each. Bligh stood rigid as he ordered the first man to strip; then he was tied to the grating by wrists and knees. The crime, and its punishment, was then announced. No one in the *Bounty* actually described the flogging; the scene was too ordinary, everyone knew what a flogging was like. But it has been described, and best described, by recruits to the Navy who were seeing it for the first time. A man might remain silent for the first half-dozen strokes, then each succeeding stroke would bring an "Oh!" or an "Oh, my God!" After a great many strokes, "his back resembles so much putrified liver, and every stroke of the cat brings away the congealed blood; and the boatswain's mates are looked at with the eye of a hawk to see that they do their duty, and clear the cat's tails after every stroke, the blood at the time streaming through their fingers . . ." Yet another account states specifically that after two dozen lashes—the number which was to be inflicted on Millward and Muspratt—"the lacerated back looks inhuman; it resembles roasted meat burnt nearly black before a scorching fire."

And what did it feel like? We know that, too. "I felt an astounding sensation between the shoulders under my neck, which went to my toenails in one direction, and my fingernails in another, and stung me to the heart, as if a knife had gone through my body . . . He came on a second time a few inches lower, and then I thought the former stroke was sweet and agreeable compared with that one . . . I felt my flesh quiver in every nerve, from the scalp of my head to my toenails. The time between each stroke seemed so long as to be agonising, and yet the next came too soon . . . The pain in my lungs was more severe, I thought, than on my back. I felt as if I would burst in the internal parts of my body . . . I put my tongue between my teeth, held it there, and bit it almost in two pieces. What with the blood from my tongue, and my lips, which I had also bitten, and the blood from my lungs, or some other internal part, ruptured by the writhing agony, I was almost choked, and became black in the face . . . The time since they began was like a long period of life; I felt as if I had lived all the time of my real life in pain and torture, and that the time when existence had pleasure in it was a dream, long, long gone by."

Twelve for Churchill, twenty-four for Millward, twenty-four for Muspratt. And, on February 4, the scarcely-healed wounds to be lividly opened again: twelve for Churchill, twenty-four for Millward, twenty-four for Muspratt. In the interval of waiting for the torture to be renewed, the three men wrote a desperate letter to Bligh, begging his forgiveness and asking him to remit the rest of the punishment. Bligh brushed it contemptuously aside. They knew the penalty for desertion; they must suffer it to the full. He was determined to have his crew in hand again. Even before the writhing men had been taken down, he had threatened every soul on board with the same punishment. Livid and raving, waving his arms about uncontrollably, a caricature of a naval officer, Bligh in his full dress uniform shouted across the bloody deck at the silent crew lined up before him. By evening, he had calmed down, had almost forgotten the matter, observing coolly in the log: "As this affair was solely caused by the neglect of the officers who had the watch I was induced to give them all a lecture on this occasion and endeavoured to show them that however exempt they were at present from the like punishment, yet they were equally subject by the Articles of War to a condign one."

Within a matter of days, Bligh had again ordered a man to have twenty-four lashes. He was continually blaming his men, and had flogged several, for being so careless as to allow the natives to steal from them. In this case the seaman, Isaac Martin, probably afraid of suffering the torture of the cat, had tried to get the article back, and, in the process, had struck a native. But this was not to Bligh's liking either. "It was," he wrote, "so violent a transgression among these friendly people and so great a violation of my orders, without any real cause but a supposition that the native had stolen a piece of iron hoop from him." The Tahitians, however, led by Tinah, were horrified at the thought of the punishment to be inflicted, and anxiously asked Bligh not to carry it out. To oblige, Bligh reduced the sentence to nineteen lashes.

On February 4, as ordered, Churchill, Millward and Muspratt were again tied up and flogged. According to Morrison, Bligh had contemplated flogging Hayward as well, but had finally decided that a long term in irons would suffice. It was this which sparked off the mysterious affair of February 6.

Bligh and Morrison tell the same story. The former wrote, "At daylight we discovered that the cable, by which the ship rode, had been cut near the water's edge, in such a manner, that only one strand remained whole." Morrison, who would have made a much better journalist than Bligh, is more exact· "Two strands of the small bower cable were observed to be cut through at the water's edge, but as the cable hung slack under the bottom, it was not observed till a squall from the westward brought it to bear ahead, when we hove it in and spliced it before the wind became sufficiently strong to part it." This was by far the most serious incident yet. The *Bounty,* lying only 100 yards from the shore, might have been wrecked and Bligh ignominiously marooned with his bread-fruit. Who had cut the cable? Wild stories began to circulate in the ship.

Bligh was firm in his opinion. "My suspicions fell chiefly, I may say wholly, on the strangers that came to us from other parts of the island; for we had on every occasion, received such unreserved and unaffected marks of good will from the people of Matavai and Oparre, that in my own mind I entirely acquited them." However, "while we were securing the ship, Tinah came on board. I could not but believe he was perfectly innocent of the transaction, nevertheless, I spoke to him in a very preremptory manner and insisted upon his discovering and bringing me the offender. The anger which I expressed, however, created so much alarm, that old Otow and his wife (the father and mother of Tinah) immediately quitted Oparre and retired to the mountains in the midst of heavy rain, as did Teppahoo and his family." Apparently, Bligh was something of an actor, with a firm belief that impressive bullying got best results. Long afterwards, he had second thoughts on the matter, saying: "It has since occurred to me that this attempt to cut the ship adrift was most probably the act of some of our own people; whose purpose of remaining at Otaheite might have been effectually answered, without danger, if the ship had been driven ashore. At the time, I entertained not the least thought of this kind."

According to Morrison, the opinions held by the officers and crew were conflicting. "This gave rise to many opinions and strict inquirey was made, but no person on board could give any account of it, tho it was the private opinion of men as well as officers that no native had been so bold as to attempt it, tho some supposed they had, as the buoy was sunk, thinking to be well paid for their trouble in diving after it. However, this remained a profound secret." There are, curiously, few observations on the skin-diving abilities of the natives; presumably, the work being so far out of their line, the seamen took no notice and certainly did not try to emulate them. Morrison's statement, however, gives some clue to their abilities. As the *Bounty* lay in 8½ fathoms (51 feet), the natives would have had to swim down that distance—a good performance, but not in itself exceptional—and *then* raise the buoy. Clearly, the Tahitians were very good divers. And, as Morrison learned later, during his long stay on the island, the attacker had in fact been a native frogman—operating, presumably, without aid from mask or flippers.

When at last Morrison learned the truth, it was at first hand. "Wyetooa, who had been Mr. Hayward's friend, told us that it was by his order that the cable was cut at Oparre. He being angry with Lieut. Bligh for putting Mr. Hayward in irons; and said if Mr. Hayward had been punished with Churchill, Muspratt and Millward, that he would have killed Lieut. Bligh, haveing taken station behind him arm'd with a clubb for that purpose. On his describing the circumstances, we recollected seeing him on board and close by Lieut. Bligh on that day. He said that as soon as he had seen Mr. Hayward receive the first blow, he intended to level the Lieut. and escape by jumping overboard, and diving till he reach'd the shore, which he said he could reach in one dive and be out of sight before anyone could know who it was that had done it." As the *Bounty* lay half a cable's length from the shore, Wyetooa seems to have been confident that he could manage 100 yards submerged on one breath—an extremely good, but not impossible, performance. As Bligh had not, in fact, flogged Hayward but had instead confined him, the Tahitian had decided to wreck the *Bounty,* so as "to get his friend out of Mr. Bligh's power, as he supposed that all hands would be forced to live on shore if the ship received much damage. He cursed Mr. Christian for not killing Lieut. Bligh which he said he would do himself if ever he came again to Taheite."

Bligh never knew how near he had come to being "levelled".

On March 2, when the night was very dark, there were some minor thefts from the post established on shore to guard the breadfruit plants; they were a watercask, part of an azimuth compass, and the bedding from Mr. Peckover's hammock. All but the bedding were recovered by Tinah, and the thief with them. The chief brought them all to Bligh, saying: "There is the thief, kill him"; pointing out that he had seen Bligh mercilessly flog his own people for any trifling offence against the natives—a reference to the nineteen lashes inflicted on Isaac Martin—and that, therefore, a Tahitian who had offended should also be punished. But Bligh's mind was a weathercock. There is no reliance to be placed on his expressed views, for now, despite his fair-sounding sentiments, he imposed an astoundingly savage sentence on the wretched native. He had him brought on board, and "punished with a hundred lashes, severely given, and from thence into irons. He bore it surprizingly and only asked me twice to forgive him altho he expected he was to die." The lashes were "severely given", but Bligh goes on to add, astonishingly,

"His back became very much swelled, but only the last stroke broke the skin." It all sounds very judicial, but Morrison's account shows Bligh going ashore, telling the officers in charge of the shore post that they had neglected their duty, and then seeking out Tinah, in a passion of temper, and demanding the instant ferreting out of the thief for punishment on board the *Bounty*. And on board the *Bounty* the wretched man remained, in irons, his back cut to ribbons, "a hostage for the good behaviour of others for the future," as Bligh put it. But he did not long remain so.

Five days later, on March 7, he escaped. "In the middle watch," wrote Bligh, "the native who I had in irons found means to break the lock of the bilboa bolt and escape about 4 o'clock in the morning. The officer of the fore castle watch heard the plunge into the water and went off in a boat in search of him to no effect." Bligh saw in this not a brilliant essay in escapeology, but dereliction of duty. "I had given written orders," he added, "that the mate of the watch was to be answerable for the prisoners and to visit and see that they were safe in his watch, but I have such a neglectful set about me that I believe nothing but condign punishment can alter their conduct. Verbal orders in the course of a month were so forgot that they would impudently assert no such orders or directions were given and I have been at last under the necessity to trouble myself with writing what by decent young officers would be complied with as the Common Rules of the Service. Mr. Stewart was the mate of the watch."

Mr. Stewart was Bligh's own choice, along with others of the "neglectful set" he had about him. Either Bligh was incapable of choosing his subordinates, or incapable of handling them. There is only one man who takes responsibility for slackness in a ship, and that is the captain. Bligh knew that, only too well was he aware of it; his long entries can be read, almost throughout, as self-defence; and that is what they probably were.

The *Bounty* had now been so long in her anchorage at Tahiti that, as the modern saying goes, she was almost aground on her spam cans. But the idea behind the phrase is not modern; it was common in Bligh's day, when seamen joked that they "expected the ship to strike upon her beef bones." There seems to be no reason why she should not have gone frequently for a cruise round the islands, exploring and charting, giving the men the feel of a heaving deck again, getting them into trim for the long passage home via the West Indies, and using the sea breeze to blow away some at least of the ill-feeling and bad temper which had plagued her all the time she had lain moored by the shore. Instead, Bligh had tried to prevent the disintegration of discipline with the lash both of his tongue and of the cat; and had failed. Hayward—the friend of the family—below in irons; Stewart—brought aboard by Bligh's influence—in disgrace; Christian—Bligh's favourite, promoted by Bligh—in a fury with his captain, because Bligh, in an incautious aside, had told a native that Christian was of no account, merely Bligh's servant; the senior warrant officers—Fryer, Purcell, Cole—nursing greater or lesser grievances; Quintal, Williams, Adams, Lamb, Thompson, Churchill, Martin, Millward, Muspratt—flogged, and filled with hatred.

By March 27, an indefinable air of sadness lay over the ship, affecting both the crew and the natives ashore. The breadfruit plants were being brought on board, and obvious preparations made for sailing. The Tahitians became more than ordinarily kind. Tinah had two *parais,* or mourning dresses, made as a present for King George; they were put on public display and a prayer recited, in which the King of England was asked to remain Tinah's friend and never to forget him. By April 1—All Fools Day—Bligh had to all intents and purposes completed his mission; the whole of the 1,015 breadfruit plants were aboard, and in a very healthy state for transplantation. The trade winds were now favourable for a fast passage to the West Indies, where Bligh would hand over his cargo to the grateful planters; and then sail for England where, he had been assured, his triumph would be rewarded by the coveted promotion from the somewhat lowly rank of Lieutenant to the awe-inspiring dignity of a Post Captain. His next command would be more imposing than the little *Bounty*.

Bligh gave a farewell dinner to Tinah and his family on April 3, and as the ship was to sail early the next morning, they all slept on board. There was very little room, as the decks were crowded with parting gifts from the Tahitians—coconuts, plantains, breadfruit, hogs, and goats. "In the evening," wrote Bligh, also apparently affected by the parting, "there was no dancing or mirth on the beach, such as we had been accustomed to, but all was silent."

At daybreak on April 4, the anchors were hauled in and, as there was no wind, the boats began to tow the *Bounty* out to sea. All that day, she hung about off Tahiti with only a light breeze stirring the sails; the natives implored Bligh to spend one more night with them but, having already said his goodbyes, he felt reluctant to comply. The native canoes followed the *Bounty* slowly out to sea, and in farewell to Tinah, Bligh ordered the hands to man ship and give the ceremonial three cheers for the chief. The English voices rang strangely out across the Pacific swell, and then, her canvas reddened by the light of sunset, the *Bounty* shook out all sail and swiftly moved off into the night.

6

"*Hold your Tongue, Sir, or You Are Dead this Instant!*"

Brave the Captain was: the seamen
made a gallant crew,
Gallant sons of English freemen,
Sailors bold and true.
But they hated his oppression,
Stern he was and rash;
So for every light transgression
Doom'd them to the lash.
Day by day more harsh and cruel
Seem'd the Captain's mood.
Secret wrath like smother'd fuel
Burnt in each man's blood.
Yet he hoped to purchase glory,
Hoped to make the name
Of his vessel great in story,
Wheresoe'er he came.
So they past by capes and islands,
Many a harbour-mouth,
Sailing under palmy highlands
Far within the South.

THE *Bounty* rolled on to Huaheine, scudding under white canvas, towing a creamy wake behind her across the blue Pacific, sailing into poetry and story forever.

Westward from Huaheine, towards the Friendly Islands,

"far within the South," as Tennyson was to write, she went. On April 11, there rose up on the horizon a large island, green with trees, topped by a round conical hill; an island not marked on any chart. As another of the Lake poets, Coleridge, was to write, also almost certainly with the *Bounty* in mind:

> The fair breeze blew, the white foam flew,
> The furrow followed free;
> We were the first that ever burst
> Into that silent sea.

Next day, April 12, Bligh entered in the log: "Punished John Sumner with 12 Lashes for neglect of duty." For the last time, the blood-stained thongs fell upon the writhing back of a seaman of the *Bounty*. Now, "secret wrath like smother'd fuel burnt in each man's blood." On April 23, Bligh anchored off the island of Annamooka; on April 25, he sent wooding and watering parties ashore, the latter under the command of Fletcher Christian.

The net was beginning to gather round Bligh. Up to now, there had been only two diarists in the ship—Bligh himself and Morrison.* From this point on, the evidence comes from all sides. John Fryer's Journal opens on April 4, and continues to the end. John Adams (alias Alexander Smith) gave his version many years later on Pitcairn Island. Peter Heywood, the midshipman, wrote a long account. Man after man of the crew, guilty and innocent, gave evidence at the court martial of the mutineers. Edward Christian, Fletcher's brother, also interviewed many of the crew, in the presence of a number of distinguished witnesses. And it all fits, even Bligh's account, as given in the log. His published account, however, was more discreet and less detailed.

Christian's agony of mind is first recorded on April 21, when the *Bounty* was still working her way between the

* Unless as Du Rietz suggests, Morrison's account was written after his return to England.

islands and Bligh was putting the crew through various exercises. Bligh now found fault with the favourite whom he had promoted. "Mr. Bligh and Mr. Christian had some words," wrote Fryer, "when Mr. Christian told Mr. Bligh 'Sir, your abuse is so bad that I cannot do my duty with any Pleasure. I have been in hell for weeks with you.' Several other disagreeable words past which had been frequently the case in the course of the voyage." Edward Christian was to collect a sample of those words, which, according to his witnesses, were used by Bligh indiscriminately to describe his officers. The choice epithets were "scoundrels, damned rascals, hounds, hell-hounds, beasts and infamous wretches."

Bligh himself recorded, on April 25, the day he sent Christian ashore with a watering party, what he then thought of them: "as to the officers I have no resource, or do I ever feel myself safe in the few instances I trust to them." The fault was in himself—he had given contradictory orders and, in his inflamed mood, Christian had told him so. "To the waterers I ordered arms," recorded Bligh, "but to be kept in the boat, and there only to be used, considering them much safer on shore without them, unless I could have encreased the party." But, he added, "To these people I not only gave my orders, but my advice; that they were to keep themselves unconnected with the natives; they however, had not been an hour on shore before one man had lost his axe and the other an adz. The cause of this was, that the officer (Christian) had, contrary to my direct orders, suffered the Indians to crowd round them and amuse them, and by that means the theft was committed." But the shore parties were small, as Bligh admits, and, according to Morrison, the situation had become ugly. The natives were not Tahitians. They became "so troublesome that Mr. Christian found it difficult to carry on the duty; he informed Lieut. Bligh of this, who damn'd him for a cowardly rascal, asking him if he was afraid of a set of naked savages while he had arms; to which Mr. Christian answer'd 'the arms are no use while your orders prevent them from being used.' "

Next day, April 26, there was a repetition of this affair. Bligh, impatient with what he thought the slowness of Christian's working party, turned to Fryer and ordered him, in Fryer's words, "to take the large cutter and go on shore and hurry Mr. Christian off with the launch." The watering place was up in the woods, about a quarter of a mile from the beach. As Fryer went in among the trees, he saw Matthew Quintal rolling a water cask down to the beach with a number of natives crowding about him. Fryer thought it best to stay with Quintal. Then, when they had loaded the cask into the boat, both together went to the watering place. There were natives all around them, and suddenly Fryer heard Quintal shout: "Mr. Fryer, there's a man going to knock you down with his club." Fryer turned round in astonishment, and, as he did so, the native lowered the club and ran off among the trees. "I was not arm'd even with a stik," wrote Fryer, feelingly. "When I came to the watering place," he went on, "Mr. Christian was getting the water filled as fast as he could, but there was a number of natives about him, some heaving stones frequently, and one chief with a very long spear frequently point'd at Mr. Christian who was arm with a Muskit and Bayonet. I then order'd Mr. Christian to git the casks down to the Boat empty or full."

When they reached the beach, they found that the boat's crew, instead of keeping the boat fended off with oars, had let go a grapnel to hold it on the beach; and, while they had been distracted by the antics of the native children, who were swimming and diving around the boat like small dolphins, the crew of a native canoe had stolen the grapnel and made off. "I then went off with the Boat," wrote Fryer, "and told Mr. Bligh what had happened. He was very warm about the loss of the Grapnail and said that he would have it again or he would detain some of the chiefs onboard untill it was brought back." Fryer pointed out that it was hardly worth while detaining natives who were already on board the *Bounty* trading with the crew as they could have had nothing to do with it; then he added, incautiously, that there were more grapnels aboard and, anyway, they had plenty of iron with which to make a new one, therefore their loss was not very great. At that, Bligh exploded.

"The loss not very great, sir. By God! sir, if it is not great to you it is great to me."

Shortly afterwards, he told Fryer to hoist the anchor and set sail. Fryer went forward to obey, and see to the stowage of the anchor. The fore topmast staysail was being let out, the ship was beginning to move, and two seamen were busy loosing the foretopsail, when Bligh roared out from the quarter-deck: "Hand the arms up!" Fryer came hurrying aft to see what was the matter, but not quickly enough for Bligh. "Why don't you come to assist me, sir! !" he barked. "Get the arms up, sir!"

The muskets were handed up and distributed to the seamen, who handled them with obvious and understandable clumsiness, as it was months since Bligh had last given them arms drill. Brandishing the weapons awkwardly, they rounded up the native chiefs who were still aboard, and drove them down below to the mess room, where, wrote Morrison, "Mr. Bligh followed them and set them to peel coconuts for his dinner. The chiefs seemed much displeased." But they were not so displeased as Bligh was. "He then came up and dismissed all the men but two, that were under arms, (but not till he had passed the compliment on officers and men to tell them that they were a parcel of lubberly rascals and that he would be one of five who would with good sticks disarm the whole of them; and presenting a pistol at Wm. McCoy, threatened to shoot him for not paying attention)."

Eventually, Bligh let the chiefs from Annamooka go free, and the *Bounty* sailed on into the night towards the island of Tofoa. In his published book, Bligh wrote: "Thus far, the . . . voyage had advanced in a course of uninterrupted prosperity, and had been attended with many circumstances equally pleasing and satisfactory."

During the night of April 26/27, while the *Bounty* was sailing between Annamooka and Tofoa, her decks were heaped with coconuts. Each officer and man had purchased some for his own use from the natives of Annamooka, at a price of one iron nail for twenty coconuts. Bligh's own pile had been diminished by the amount he had ordered the imprisoned chiefs to peel for him, as their punishment. Perhaps he forgot this, perhaps he was just short-tempered, probably he simply wanted an opportunity to carry on his feud with Christian. But when he came on deck on the morning of April 27, he insisted that his own pile had been looted.

"Mr. Fryer," he shouted gesticulating, "don't you think those coconuts are shrunk since last night?"

Before the vehemence of the angry Bligh, the master's replies seemed lame. Yes, he admitted, it was true that the piles heaped between the guns seemed not to be so high as they had been before; indeed, he was quite certain of it, for he had had them stowed up as high as the rail. But then, the heaps of nuts might well have been upset and spread about by members of the crew on duty blundering about on deck in the darkness of the night.

Bligh would not have it. There was a passionate explosion of wrath, and he screamed for Fletcher Christian, the officer of the morning watch.

"Damn your blood," he roared, "you have stolen my coconuts!"

"I was dry," muttered Christian, "I thought it of no consequence. I took one only, and I am sure no one touched another."

"You lie, you scoundrel, you have stolen one half!" screamed Bligh, his words carrying to every man on deck.

White-faced and shaken, miserable at being shamed in front of his friends and the men he had to command, tied in the strait-jacket of service discipline which forbids a junior to answer back and virtually ties his tongue, Christian could only say wretchedly and almost inaudibly, "Why do you treat me thus, Captain Bligh?"

Bligh began to howl with passion even at this answer. He shook his hand in Christian's face, as if about to physically strike him, and screamed, "No reply!" And as Christian trembled with resentment, Bligh lashed out verbally, "You thief!" It was as pitiful a spectacle, this public humiliation of an officer, as a flogging was for a seaman . . . and, if he wished, if Christian gave him the chance by now saying so much as one word without being spoken to, Bligh could have him disrated and actually flogged. But the white-faced Christian remained silent.

That was not enough for Bligh, he wanted more resentment to cut his teeth on. "Master at Arms!" he bawled.

"Sir!"

"Master at Arms, see that every coconut which is below is brought on deck. Bring them all up. Everybody's!" And he screamed out again, "Everybody's!"

There was dead silence on deck. They were all to be treated as criminals, from the oldest and most responsible officer to the most thoughtless of young seamen. As the coconuts were being brought up and taken aft, and all the officers and men assembled, Bligh was barking at the officers. The coconuts could not have been stolen without their knowledge, he declared. There was a chorus of denial; all the officers without exception replying that they had not seen a single man touch a coconut.

"Then you must have taken them yourselves," screamed Bligh.

When the piles of coconuts were complete, Bligh began to question their owners, starting with Edward Young, a midshipman. "How many nuts did you buy, Mr. Young?" Young told him.

"And how many did you eat?"

"I don't know, sir."

"Don't know, sir!"

"This is the remainder, sir, but I haven't counted them."

One by one, Bligh passed down the line of officers, barking out the same questions. Tension rose as he drew nearer to Fletcher Christian. This was what Bligh was waiting for, making his former favourite sweat with fear. At length, he was looking Christian in the face.

"Mr. Christian, how many nuts did you buy?"

"I do not know, sir, but I hope you don't think me so mean as to be guilty of stealing yours?"

The answer, bold in the circumstances, once more set Bligh off in a blaze.

"Yes, you dam'd hound, I do! You must have stolen them from me or you could give a better account of them."

Then he stepped back and shouted at all the officers collectively. "God damn you, you scoundrels, you are all thieves alike, and combine with the men to rob me! I suppose you'll steal my yams next," he jeered. Then, raising his voice, "But I'll sweat you for it, you rascals. I'll make the half of you jump overboard before you get through Endeavour Straits! I take care of you now for my own good, but when I get you through the Straits, you may all go to hell! If you do not look sharp, I shall do for one half of you—I'll leave you in Jamaica —you shall not go home with me—" The half-incoherent threats tumbled out, while like a madman—but dressed in the blue and gold of His Majesty's service—he shook his fist at them and waved his arms about. Then he screamed, "Mr. Samuel!"

Samuel came running up.

"Stop these villains' grog and give them but half a pound of yams tomorrow, and if they steal then, I'll reduce them to a quarter!"

The parade was then dismissed and the coconuts taken below, while the officers gathered in a group and, according to Morrison, "were heard to murmur much at such treatment". That is, they were now openly criticising their captain in front of the crew; and the crew also were disturbed. "It was talked among the men that the yams would next be seized, as Lieut. Bligh knew that they had purchased large quantitys of them; and they set about secreting as many as they could of their own." Virtually everyone in the ship, except possibly Mr. Samuel, was now an open enemy of Bligh, with fresh wounds or resentments to remember; Bligh had turned command into a contest once again. But still, he was not satisfied. He had not sufficiently humiliated Christian, the man's spirit was still not quite broken. He was not able to relax until, that afternoon, the job was done.

After Bligh had been screaming at him, Christian was seen to literally run forward from the quarterdeck, his face contorted, sobbing openly. They were tears of humiliated pride and frustrated, powerless rage—for Christian was as highly-strung as Bligh. Purcell, the carpenter, one of Bligh's oldest opponents, sympathetically asked Christian what was the matter.

"Can you ask me, and hear the treatment I receive?"

"Do I not receive as bad as you do?" said Purcell, encouragingly.

"You have something to protect you and can speak again," said Christian bitterly, "but if I should speak to him as you do, he would probably break me, turn me before the mast, and perhaps flog me." Then self-pity turned to ungovernable rage. "If he did, it would be the deaths of us both, for I am sure I should take him in my arms and jump overboard with him."

"Never mind," said Purcell, "it is but for a short time longer."

"No, no—in going through Endeavour Straits, I am sure the ship will be a hell."

The Straits were difficult and dangerous for navigation,

where a slight error could have fatal consequences; there would be every opportunity, there, for Bligh to pounce on the slightest apparent slackness or mistake in judgement. The whole atmosphere of the ship would be unbearably tense from the nervous professional anxiety of their captain; and the tension would go on for days, even weeks, for the passage was a lengthy one.

Christian was in receipt of general sympathy from his comrades in the ship. The boatswain, William Cole, told him to "keep his heart up."

"To be counted a thief is more than I can bear," was Christian's sullen reply.

"I would rather die ten thousand deaths than bear this treatment," he told another friend. "I always do my duty as an officer and as a man ought to do, yet I receive this scandalous usage."

Although Bligh was careful not to log these incidents—if he had, his commission might well have been terminated—he was later faced with Morrison's account (sent to him by Banks), and had to think up a reply. In it, he accused all the officers of having permitted the coconuts to be stolen; "here," he wrote, "was a publick theft; a contumacy, & direct disobedience of orders." In his concluding sentence, he skirted cautiously round what could have been a court-martial charge for him. "The particular offenders could not be found out . . . could therefore either the epithet Thief or Villain, had it been used, have justified their taking the ship the next day?" He will not exactly say that he called anyone a thief or villain, and he will not mention at all the crux of the matter: that he abused all of the officers in front of all of the men. That he had no proof at all, is beside the point; had he been able to prove it up to the hilt, he still would not have been justified in doing what, in every service, in every country of the world, in any age, is simply not done—and for very good reasons.

The most astounding thing about Bligh's conduct on this

day is that, about an hour after having reduced Christian to tears by his second outburst of abuse—Bligh invited Christian to have dinner with him in his cabin that night. Or perhaps it is not so strange. He had got what he wanted, broken the spirit of his former ship's favourite—or so he thought. But Christian excused himself from accepting that curious invitation by saying that he was feeling unwell. Hearing of this, and expecting that Bligh would invite someone else, the officers got together and agreed that, in view of his conduct towards them that day, no officer would accept an invitation to meet their captain socially. The officer Bligh chose, however, was the rather unpleasant senior midshipman, Thomas Hayward—the man he had punished for being asleep on watch. The wretched youngster, torn between fear of his messmates, fear of his captain, and fear for his own career, hesitated a moment—and then accepted. As he walked to Bligh's cabin that night, there was an ominous sound in the ship; the other officers were hissing him.

Meanwhile, the actions of Fletcher Christian were odd and unaccountable. First, he gave away all the native curios he had collected as souvenirs to bring home to England. Then, he was seen in the forechains, tearing up letters and papers, and throwing the fragments overboard. Soon, he had no personal impedimenta left in the ship. Finally, he sought out Purcell, the carpenter, and asked for some nails; Purcell let him take as many as he pleased from the locker. Christian was going to desert on a home-made raft, rather than face the rest of the voyage with Bligh.

He afterwards told Morrison that "he had determined to quit the ship, and had informed the boatswain, carpenter, and two midshipmen (Stewart and Hayward) of his intention to do so; that by them he was supplied with part of a roasted pig, some nails, beads, and other articles of trade, which he put into a bag that was given him by the last-named gentleman; that he put this bag into the clue of Robert Tinkler's hammock, where it was discovered by that young gentleman when going to bed at night but the business was smothered."

On deck, Fryer, who had the first watch, noted that the weather cleared at about 10 P.M. and there was bright moonlight. He then saw Bligh come on deck to leave his Orders for the Night. "We at that time was upon speaking terms—but I am sorry to say that that was but sildom," Fryer quaintly observed in his Journal. So he now spoke to his captain.

"Sir, there is a breeze springing up fair and a young moon, which will be lucky for us to come on the coast of New Holland."

"Yes, Mr. Fryer, so it will," observed Bligh, gave his Night Orders, and departed.

At midnight, Mr. Peckover, the gunner, took the watch from Fryer. Christian was to relieve Peckover at 4 A.M. He would then have his chance to get his raft over the side and be well away to the nearest land, some seven or eight miles distant, before his absence was noticed. Still, Christian hung about late on deck that night, impatient to be away earlier still, if an opportunity occurred. But, away across the still, dark water, where the land lay, a distant volcano was in eruption; and men were continually coming on deck to watch the spectacle. Eventually he went below and lay down. It seemed that he had only just dropped off, when the midshipman, George Stewart, was shaking him awake to take over the 4 A.M. watch. Bleary-eyed, sleepless, nerve-ridden, Christian seemed to Stewart—who knew of his plan to escape—"much out of order," and in no fit state for so desperate a venture. He begged him earnestly to abandon his intention of swimming, supported by only a plank and some staves. But Christian had whipped himself up to a state of desperation, in which considerations of his own safety could have no part. He started to pull on his disordered clothing.

"There's no need to swim," said Stewart, savagely. "The people are ripe for anything!"

A European sailor in a Pacific island village. From an old print. *Photo: Alexander McKee*

A contemporary artist's impression of the mutineers allowing the *Bounty's* launch to be stocked with provisions. From an old print. *Photo: Alexander McKee*

Souvenirs of the open boat voyage: the gourd, cup, bullet-weight and rough logbook which Bligh used. From an old print. *Photo: Alexander McKee*

An accurate replica of the *Bounty's* launch being built at the Maritime Workshop, Gosport, in 1988. The original was constructed by J. Samuel White of Cowes, Isle of Wight, probably at their Gosport yard, where the present workshop is sited. *Photo: Alexander McKee, by permission of the William Bligh Trust*

Christian stopped a moment, thunderstruck, then went on deck, looking thoughtful. In his frenzied state of mind, to think was to act. And this time every factor was favourable, and everything went exactly right. It was quite breath-takingly easy.

The unspeakable Hayward, who was mate of the watch and whom Christian rigidly ignored, was overcome by his usual sleepiness and lay down on an arms chest; despite his recent memory of being in irons for the same lapse, he was soon snoring gently. Little Tom Ellison, aged 17, and only 5 feet 3 inches tall, was at the wheel; John Mills, the gunner's mate, was conning the ship; Thomas Burkett was keeping a lookout forward. There was no sign of Hallet, the other midshipman; naturally enough, as he also was asleep on an arms chest, that in the main hatchway. The first two seamen to whom Christian spoke were Matthew Quintal and Isaac Martin, both of them flogged by Bligh for trivialities. Agreement was a matter of moment only; with fierce joy on their faces they went in search of those of their shipmates who, they were certain, would assist them. While Christian returned to his post, they were below, waking the chosen men from their sleep. Matthew Thompson, John Adams, John Williams, Charles Churchill—they had all tasted the cat and all they wanted now were weapons. William M'Coy, whom Bligh had threatened to pistol only a few days before, they also woke; and M'Coy was as eager as the rest. Then they sent Churchill on deck, to confer with Christian as to how they were to get hold of the arms.

At about 5 A.M., an hour after Christian's watch had come on duty, little Tom Ellison saw Churchill come on deck and go over to Christian, who was standing alone on the starboard side of the quarter-deck. The *Bounty* was then heeled over on the starboard tack, the water gurgling blackly past her sides and the wake shimmering with phosphorescence behind her. "Churchill spook to Mr. Christian in Close Conversation about ten Minutes," recalled Ellison. "I could not hear one word that past between them, they being a breast of the foremust gun, on the qr. deck."

Shortly afterwards, there was a shout from forward. "There's a shark on the larboard quarter!" The call came from one of the men on watch, Charles Norman, the carpenter's mate. That woke Hayward and Hallet, and the two midshipmen became greatly excited at the sight of the enormous creature. Hayward called out to Norman, "Don't make a noise!" and Hallet ran forward along the larboard side of the deck, calling out for someone to get a hook. Christian acted with speed and decision to take advantage of this great opportunity. Saying that he was going to get a musket and shoot the beast, he ran down the fore hatchway, and quickly opened the arms chest. In a moment, six of the mutineers were armed with muskets and bayonets; they poured up on deck, loading as they went. After them came Christian, with a drawn cutlass. M'Coy stopped running for a moment, to thump the deck with the butt of his musket, shouting: "Bear a hand, for Mr. Hayward is gone aft to tell the captain!" The little knot of armed men passed the bewildered Hallet who, when he tried to get down the hatchway, was prevented by a newly-posted sentinel. Hayward, astounded at all this fuss about a shark, for he had not in fact gone down below, called out to Christian; and was told to hold his tongue. Then the whole lot—Churchill, Burkett, Sumner, Quintal, M'Coy, Martin, Adams, Hillbrant and perhaps Mills also—went pouring down the after hatchway in the wake of Christian, to where Bligh's cabin was. Then, a moment later, above the commotion there was the familiar voice of their captain—but this time, with a new note in it. "Murder!" he screamed.

Then Christian's voice, unrecognisable with fury: "Hold your tongue, sir, or you are dead this instant!"

7

"*Too Late, Captain Bligh*"

"AT DAWN OF DAY," wrote Bligh in his report to the Admiralty, "Fletcher Christian, Officer of the Watch, Chas. Churchill (Ship's Corporal), Thos. Burkett (Seaman), John Mills (Gunner's Mate), came into my Cabbin, and while I was asleep, seized me in my Bed, and tied my hands behind my back with a strong Cord, and with Cutlasses and Bayonets fixed at my Breast, threatened instant death if I spoke or made the least Noise. I nevertheless called out so loud for help that everyone heard me and were flying to my assistance, but all my Officers except those who were concerned found themselves secured by armed Centinels." The truth was otherwise. Not an officer or man lifted a finger to help Bligh, let alone went "flying to his assistance."

At the subsequent court martial seventeen of the *Bounty's* crew gave detailed, voluminous, scattered, but not too contradictory evidence as to how the ship was taken; some scenes are vague, others quite clear; the sequence is not absolutely certain, for a great many happenings were taking place almost at the same time, and sometimes simultaneously. Swift patterns of movement formed and dissolved again; but certain scenes stayed in the minds of particular witnesses.

Fryer, whose cabin was opposite Bligh's, was woken up at more or less the same time as Bligh, but more gently. As he started up, Sumner and Quintal put a hand on his chest, and said, "Sir, you are a prisoner." Fryer opened his mouth for an indignant reply, but they told him to hold his tongue. "But if you make yourself quiet, sir, there is no one on board will hurt a hair of your head." Raising himself up, Fryer saw Bligh being forced up the ladder, his hands tied behind him, and clad only in his shirt.

In his logbook, but not in his best-selling book, Bligh took note of that moment also. "The master's cabbin was opposite to mine—He saw them (the pistols in Bligh's cabin) for our eyes met each other through his door window, and he had a pair of ships pistols loaded with ammunition in his cabbin. A firm resolution might have made a good use of them." But Fryer was unlikely to take a risk for a man whom he detested and with whom he had rarely been on speaking terms; and, anyway, his pistols were useless, as there was no ammunition with them—according to Fryer's statement, which contradicts Bligh's. A moment afterwards, Churchill burst into Fryer's cabin and, seizing the pistols and Fryer's cutlass, said: "I'll take care of these."

"What are you going to do with your captain?" Fryer asked Sumner and Quintal, both of whom bore the marks of Bligh's lash on their backs.

"Damn his eyes," said Sumner, "put him in the boat, and let the bugger see if he can live upon three fourths of a pound of yams a day."

"Into the boat?" burst out Fryer, "For Godsake for what?"

"O hold your tongue," snapped one of them.

"Mr. Christian is Captain of the Ship now," said the other. "Recollect, Mr. Fryer, that Mr. Bligh has brought all this upon himself."

"Consider, my lads, what you are about," pleaded Fryer, who could only too well foresee the dreadful consequences for them. There was no other penalty than death for the crime of mutiny.

"We know very well what we are about," they replied.

Elsewhere in the ship, there were equally startled awakenings. Had the plan been long and carefully prepared, some news of it might have leaked out; as it was, Stewart's involuntary prompting of Christian, and Christian's hasty, almost instantaneous decision to change his plot to escape into an attempt to capture the *Bounty,* resulted in complete surprise. The ship was his, without a shot being fired or a blow struck.

Christian's right-hand man in all this had been Charles Churchill, the ship's corporal, whose back was scarred by the 24 lashes which he had received in two terrible instalments. In his dread of the second dose, he had humbly written to Bligh, thanking him for not trying him by court martial and begging him to remit the final 12 lashes. "We trust our future conduct will fully remonstrate our deep sense of your clemency, and our stedfast resolution to behave better hereafter," he had written on behalf of himself, Muspratt, and Millward. Now, he was a demon of driving efficiency in the take-over of the *Bounty.*

When Hayward, astounded, had first seen the men with muskets come on deck, Churchill had delayed any action the midshipman might have taken to warn Bligh by stating, casually, "Yes, I don't know the Captain's reason for it, he has order'd to Exercise at day light."

Like lightning, Williams had gone onto the forecastle with a musket, while M'Coy stood by the fore hatchway, thumping the coaming with his musket butt and shouting, "Bear a hand up." Mills and other mutineers had taken over the quarter-deck and were standing beside Tom Ellison at the wheel. There had been a sound of breaking glass from below, and shouts of: "Mr. Fryer, stay in your cabin!" and, "Mr. Nelson, stay below!" They had needed rope with which to tie Bligh's hands before bringing him on deck, and Churchill had seen to that too. He broke into the startled confusion with: "Hand down a seizing to tie the captain's hands." And when nobody moved, he had got instant action by roaring: "You infernal buggers, hand down a seizing or I'll come up and play hell with you all." One of the lead lines was immediately cut, and handed down below.

Hayward had never even made a move to warn Bligh. Christian, in passing, had shaken a cutlass in his face, snarling: "Damn your blood, Hayward, mamoo." Tahitian words had become catch-phrases in the ship; this one meant "Hold your tongue." And the terrified Hayward had.

Mr. Peckover, the gunner, had been awakened by confused noises and what he thought was the sound of bayonets being fixed. He had jumped out of bed, hurriedly put on his trousers, and met Nelson, the quiet and inoffensive botanist who had charge of the breadfruit plants.

"The ship is taken," said Nelson. "It is by our own people, and Mr. Christian at their head. But we know whose fault it is."

Mr. Peckover did. He was of the same mind as Fryer and Purcell, and of the same stamp.

When the two men went to the hatchway, they were stopped by the gleaming bayonets of Quintal and Sumner. Nelson was ordered to keep below, Peckover was to come up.

All over the ship, the same scenes were happening; some men being ordered to stay below, others to come on deck, with the orders being countermanded in the utmost confusion soon after; with no one quite sure who was a mutineer and who was not—except for nine out of the ten men whom Bligh had flogged, for they were the armed, hardened, and determined core of the revolt.

Young Peter Heywood woke up to see a man with a drawn cutlass in his hand sitting on the arms chest in the main hatchway. On asking him what was happening, the seaman said that "Mr. Christian had seized the captain and put him in confinement; had taken command of the ship and meant to carry Bligh home a prisoner, in order to try him by Court Martial, for his long tyrannical and oppressive conduct."

Such was the inevitable confusion of a hastily contrived mutiny; in any other ship, it might speedily have been counterattacked and beaten down, smothered almost at birth. But no one was prepared to risk anything for Bligh; indeed, there was a great sense of relief, and some of the young seamen, like Ellison, who had not been let into the secret even at the last minute, were jumping with joy, running about and clapping their hands delightedly at the downfall and humiliation of the tyrant. "Damn him, I will be centinel over him," said the lad.

But Ellison's first reaction had been shock at the sudden change of fortune. As he testified at court martial: "I was surprised to see Mr. Christian and Party come upon Deck bringing up Captn. Bligh in his shirt with his hands tide behind him; this Proceeding greatly amaz'd and Terrifyde me; my terror was more Increas'd, at the site of Mr. Christian; he looked like a Madman, is long hair was luse, is shirt Collair open." With one hand, Christian held one end of the rope which was securing Bligh's hands behind his back, with the other he was waving a bayonet in his captain's face. Bligh, his face contorted with fury, was shouting insults and defiance as he was forced over towards the mizen mast, his shirt tails flapping in the breeze, for they had not given him time to put on his trousers. Churchill gave him a shove to help him on his way, and two men—John Adams and Thomas Burkett—were set to guard him with loaded muskets and fixed bayonets. Bligh's cries of rage brought a savage snarl from Christian: "Mammoo, Sir, mammoo!" Then he turned away to give orders to Tom Ellison at the wheel, and Ellison instantly obeyed. Christian was captain of the *Bounty*.

It was too much for Bligh. He started to rage again, but the violent reaction of the mutineers brought him instantly to his senses. There were harsh shouts of "Damn his eyes, the bugger, blow his brains out!" And Churchill, his eyes glittering, held the point of a bayonet at Bligh's throat, and threatened him with instant death if he so much as uttered another sound.

Already, one of the boats was being swung out. Bligh's

fate was obvious. Down below, Fryer was told of this, and when he asked what boat he was to be sent away in, his guards said that it was the Jolly Boat.

"The Jolly Boat won't swim," protested Fryer, "the bottom is almost eat out with worms."

"Damn his eyes!" was the reply, "The boat is too good for him."

Fryer had a thoroughgoing hatred of Bligh, but he did not want to see him sent to his death; he argued earnestly to be allowed to go on deck and speak to Bligh. One of his guards shouted up to Christian to know if Fryer might come up, and Christian said no. But a few minutes afterwards, Christian changed his mind and allowed Fryer on deck. He found Bligh still a prisoner by the mizen mast, although one of the seamen had gone to fetch his trousers. Hayward and Hallet were standing dejectedly by the rail, in a funk obvious to every witness. Christian told them brusquely to get into the boat.

"What harm did I ever do you, Mr. Christian, that you should send me in the boat?" pleaded Hayward.

"I hope you'll not insist on it, Mr. Christian," mumbled Hallet, tears filling his eyes.

"Get into the boat," said Christian contemptuously; then he called for Samuel, Bligh's hated clerk, and ordered him into the boat also. The tight-lipped Samuel appeared quite unmoved.

The intervention of Fryer and Cole saved Bligh. Cole, the boatswain, was already on deck, having been ordered to hoist out the jolly boat, with a growled threat "to take care of himself", if he did not do it properly. Fryer's first act, when he came up from below, was to talk quietly to Christian, trying to dissuade him from his purpose. When he proved adamant, Fryer then suggested that Christian might merely put Bligh under arrest, and continue with the voyage home. "Hold your tongue, sir, I have been in hell for weeks past—Captain Bligh has brought all this on himself."

"At least give Captain Bligh a better boat than the small cutter, her bottom is almost out," pleaded Fryer. "Let him have a chance to get on shore."

"No, that boat is good enough."

Fryer went over to Bligh, and whispered that he wanted to stay on board, and in that way might soon be able to follow him. "By all means stay, Mr. Fryer," said Bligh so loudly that Christian heard. But as he took no notice, Bligh said to Fryer, "Knock Christian down, knock him down!" Apparently, Bligh had some idea that one of the armed mutineers, Isaac Martin, was really a friend. But Fryer had no opportunity to test this theory, for Christian at once ordered him taken below again. At the hatchway, he passed Morrison, who was helping with some tackle for the boat. "I hope you have had no hand in this business," said Fryer. When Morrison replied that he had not known a word about it, Fryer said quietly, "Be on your guard; there may be an opportunity of recovering ourselves."

Morrison shook his head. "Go down to your cabin, sir, it's too late."

Once below, Fryer contacted Peckover, the gunner, and Nelson, the botanist. They could hear Samuel, busy collecting Bligh's kit and papers, to be put in the boat with them. Fryer had already gathered that the mutineers had an agreement among themselves not to murder anyone, so he suggested that they all stay in the ship, in the hope of being able to recover it. Doubtless he had an incentive to stay, in the obvious unseaworthiness of the jolly boat. But Peckover grunted. "If we stay we shall be all deemed Pirates." Fryer said no, he would answer for them. He made an uncomplimentary remark about Bligh, and implied that he was not going to share his captain's fate if he could help it. He had a wife and children at home to think of. At that moment, one of the mutineers came to take Fryer on deck again. Christian said he was to go in the boat.

Now, the boat was no longer the unseaworthy jolly boat, but the *Bounty's* large launch. Cole and Purcell had gone to Christian who, frowning, had at first taken no notice of them, but had at last consented to let Bligh have the launch. "For God's sake, Mr. Cole, do all that lies in your power!" shouted Bligh from the background. Purcell butted in with: "Mr. Christian, I have done nothing that I am ashamed of, and I want to see my native country again." There was an immediate argument between Christian and Churchill, and some of the other mutineers. This was the consequence of the haste in which they had acted; they had not thought out the question, nor even considered that many of the crew might want to go with Bligh, rather than take the risk of being afterwards accused of mutiny and piracy. Now they had to decide who was to go—for some of the key technicians were essential to the working of the ship—and who was to stay, even if they wanted to go. And since many of those who wanted to go were their friends, they had to decide what they could be allowed to take with them, in the shape of clothes, food, water, navigational instruments, and weapons. Abruptly, Christian terminated the argument, turned to Purcell, and said: "Do you get the boat ready directly." While Cole went below to rout out everyone to take their places in the boat, Purcell ordered two of the seamen, McIntosh and Norman, to get him from the storeroom the gear he needed to hoist out the launch. Then, under Purcell's direction, other men began clearing the launch of various impedimenta which had been stored in it. It was very hard to tell, at this moment, who was a mutineer and who was not; and, indeed, the unspeakable Hayward—who was then so terror-stricken that everyone who saw him noticed it—was afterwards to say that one man was not a mutineer, because he helped to get the launch out, and that another man was a mutineer, because he also had helped to get the boat out. One of the mutineers, Isaac Martin, actually got into the boat, having apparently changed his mind, but was ordered out of it by his comrades.

And as it became apparent how many wanted to go in the launch, and how low in the water it would be in consequence, man after man found himself faced with the decision: go with Bligh—and sink; or go with Christian—and hang.

The third alternative—retake the ship—occurred to few. The risk was too great. Christian dominated the ship. According to Bligh, "He seemed to be plodding instant destruction on himself and every one, for of all diabolical looking men, he exceeded every possible description." And, like a tiger, Charles Churchill seconded him. He had seen Fryer speak to Morrison at the hatchway, and had come over at once to ask what he had said, shaking his cutlass with fury. "He only asked me if we were going to have the longboat," replied Morrison.

"It's a damned lie, Charlie, for I saw him and Millward shake hands when the Master spoke to them," shouted John Adams, who was standing within earshot.

Churchill turned back to Morrison. "I would have you mind how you come on, for I have my eye on you."

Adams then shouted: "Stand to your arms, for they intend to make a rush!"

That put the mutineers on guard and what was afterwards referred to by a number of the crew as "Fryer's push to retake the ship" was stillborn. In the evident confusion and intermingling, and with the hard-core mutineers so few in number—probably no more than eight or ten—it might have been done, had Bligh possessed an equal number of partisans equally determined. But "Fryer's push" never amounted to much more than talk, for it involved more than the clear case of duty versus mutiny. It meant taking the side of Bligh against Christian, when all their inclinations ran the opposite way. Christian fortified the resolution of his own side, by ordering a seaman, John Smith, to bring up a bottle of rum from Bligh's own private stock, and serve it out to his armed sentries, standing at strategic points on deck. No doubt he hoped it would make them more reckless, and forgetful of what the consequences might be. For his part, Bligh tried to rally the crew to him, shouting out incoherently and indiscriminately, until he was hoarse, when Christian snapped: "Mammoo, sir, not a word, or death's your portion."

Christian's threat, which he had no intention of carrying out, was reinforced by a threatening growl from some of the mutineers: "Blow his brains out." With the drink in them, they might have done it on impulse before Christian could stop them; and Bligh lapsed into hasty silence.

With a dozen men heaving at the ropes, the *Bounty's* launch was lifted off the deck, and swung out over the side. To Bligh, it seemed very final. At any moment, he would have to leave the *Bounty*. He was about to lose his ship, irrevocably, the ultimate disgrace for a captain; for which he would inevitably be called to account. He made a last effort to overcome Christian, talking this time reasonably and sanely, all the rage and passion sweated out of him. "Consider what you are about, Mr. Christian," he called, "for God's sake drop it and there shall be no more come of it." Christian shook his head. "'Tis too late, Captain Bligh."

"No, Mr. Christian, it is not too late yet," pleaded Bligh. "I'll forfeit my honour if I ever speak of it; I'll give you my bond that there shall never be any more come of it."

A savage note came into Christian's voice. "You know, Captain Bligh, you have treated me like a dog all the voyage. I have been in hell this fortnight past and I am determined to suffer it no longer."

Cole and Purcell joined in, urging Christian to give up the mutiny, but he shook his head. "You know, Mr. Cole, how I have been used."

"I know it very well, Mr. Christian, we all know it, but drop it, for God's sake!"

Hayward, fearful for himself, then dared to put in a word, "Consider, Mr. Christian, what a dangerous step you have taken." Christian did not trouble to answer him.

Desperately, Bligh made his final plea. "Can there be no other method taken?"

But it was Churchill who answered him, with a growl of: "No, this is the best and only method."

Now it only remained to select who was to go in the boat, and what they were to take with them. The ship needed armourers and carpenters, so Christian ordered Coleman, McIntosh, and Norman to remain; and also Michael Byrn, the half-blind Irish fiddler, by popular demand, for there were cries of, "We must not part with our fiddler." Byrn was already in the boat, by his own inclination, but Churchill soon routed him out, threatening to "send him to the Shades" if he attempted again to quit the ship. Seeing Burkett lingering nearby, Churchill told him to go aft, "and to take care of himself." "I have seen you shifting about, but I have my eye on you," he added.

Purcell got into the boat to stow his belongings. Finding Isaac Martin, one of the mutineers there, with a bag of possessions, he asked him what he thought he was doing. "I'm going in the boat," said Martin. "If ever we get to England, I'll endeavour to hang you myself," snarled Purcell. The carpenter had brought his tool chest with him, and when this was noted, there were shouts of protest. "We might as well give him the ship, he'll build another vessel in a month." The ensuing dispute confirmed Purcell's right to a seat in the boat, but Martin was hauled out of it after Churchill and Quintal had pointed their muskets at him, and some of the tools were removed from the chest. Churchill and Quintal began to cruise about, growling: "Damn them, they have enough."

As each man went down into the boat, Christian, waving a bayonet, called out, "Take care you take nothing away!" Finally, he told Churchill to get the officers off the ship. As Fryer was brought forward, he said, "Let me stay, Mr. Christian, for you'll not know what to do with the ship." But Christian replied, "We can do very well without you, Mr. Fryer." Churchill then pushed the reluctant master into the boat. The tearful Hallet and Hayward were next, begging Christian to let them stay aboard the *Bounty*. As soon as they were in it, they began to shout that it was overloaded, and to try to keep anyone else from coming into it. Bligh then shouted out unexpectedly, "For God's sake, my lads, don't overload the boat," to those who were about to get into it. And when they paused, reluctantly, he said, "I will do you justice if I ever reach England." That decided one or two, and they hung back, but asking Bligh to remember them, that they had wanted to go with him, that they were not mutineers. Bligh's hands were then untied, and he was led to the gangway. He made a last attempt to reason with Christian, referring to their former friendship, and asking him to consider his wife and family. "You should have thought of them before," replied Christian.

The impatient Churchill broke in, "Come, come, Captain Bligh, your officers are in the boat and waiting for you. You must go."

Norman and McIntosh called out to Bligh to remember that they had been kept against their will; Morrison spoke to Cole, saying that he was remaining aboard only because the boat was so low in the water. "God bless you, my boy," said Cole, "were it not for my wife and family I would stay myself."

As Bligh got into the boat, it lurched dangerously in the water, wallowing low under the extra weight. It seemed impossible that it could last for long in any sea. People were standing up or kneeling, trying to find places for themselves and their belongings; there was hardly room for them all even to sit in the launch. Bligh at once ordered some of the kit, particularly the hammocks, thrown overboard. There was a chorus of jeers from the mutineers leaning over the rail, and one or two threats. Cole asked Bligh to cast off, as he thought the mutineers might fire down into them. Bligh ignored him, but pushed the boat away from the gangway and astern of the *Bounty,* so that no more men could come into her, at the same time shouting up to some of those on board: "My lads, I will do you all justice, for I know who's who."

8

"*Hollow and Ghastly Countenances*"

THERE were nineteen men now in the launch. They were Bligh, whose command had shrunk in a few hours from a ship to a rowboat; the master, John Fryer; the boatswain, William Cole; the gunner, William Peckover; the carpenter, William Purcell; the acting surgeon, Thomas Ledward; the master's mate, William Elphinstone; the two scared midshipmen, Thomas Hayward and John Hallet; Bligh's clerk, John Samuel; the botanist, David Nelson; two quartermasters, Peter Linkletter and John Norton; the doctor's assistant, George Simpson; the sailmaker, Lawrence Lebogue; and only four able seamen—Robert Tinkler, John Smith, Thomas Hall, and Robert Lamb. The latter was the only one among them who had suffered under the lash at Bligh's orders. Under their weight, and the weight of their kit and provisions, the sides of the launch were a bare seven or eight inches above the level of the sea.

The rail of the Bounty was crowded with men, not all of them mutineers, engaged, as the fancy took them, in hooting and jeering at Bligh, or in handing down various articles which might be of use to the men who were being cast away. "Go and see if you can live on a quarter of a pound of yams a day," one of them yelled down at Bligh. "Shoot the bugger!" roared another, Richard Skinner, raising his musket.

Just in time, it was knocked aside by some other man on deck. Others called down to friends in the boat, asking them, if ever they got back to England, to tell their relatives what had happened to them. At this, some wit shouted: "Tell my friends I am somewhere in the South Seas!" There was a roar of laughter, and shouts of, "Huzza for Otaheite!"

Morrison handed down several pieces of pork to John Norton in the boat; Norton promptly fumbled it, and they went overboard. "Damn your eyes!" snarled Cole. Morrison also handed down some gourds of water, and Bligh then asked him to get them some muskets. Christian would not allow it, but let Churchill and Morrison put four cutlasses in the launch. "There, Captain Bligh!" jeered Churchill. "You don't stand in need of firearms, as you are going among your friends." Bligh asked for another word with Christian, and Christian replied by forbidding anyone on any pretext to speak to Bligh. "We'd better cast off," said Cole, "they'll do us a mischief if we stay much longer." Christian had come to the same decision, for different reasons. He had intended to tow the overloaded boat nearer to the land, before casting it off, but there was so little wind and the sea was so calm, that he remarked: "They will make better at their oars than wait to be towed." The launch was then cast off, and dropped slowly astern of the *Bounty*. They could hear Christian giving orders, and as the *Bounty* drew away from them, still on her original course as set by Bligh, they saw little Tom Ellison go up the rigging and loose the main-topgallant sail.

The launch was 23 feet long, with a beam of 6 feet 9 inches and a depth of 2 feet 9 inches. So low in the water was she, that the men could easily trail their fingers in the water. There was no inclination to do this, because soon after they had unshipped the six oars and began to row, a shark rose up under one of the oar blades, as if to strike at it. A little afterwards, they got up the foremast and set a sail on it. Then they began to take stock of the provisions, which amounted to 150 lbs. of bread, 16 pieces of pork, 6 quarters of rum, 6 bottles of wine, and 28 gallons of water. Among the documents which Samuel had managed to obtain from Bligh's cabin, was the ship's log; but there were no charts or maps. They had a compass and some navigational instruments, some of the carpenter's tools, and four cutlasses; there were no firearms. The island of Tofoa was on the horizon, and they steered for that, hoping to pick up more supplies.

They also took stock, now and later, of what had happened to them and why; and what was likely to be their fate. They were more than 3,000 miles from the nearest European settlement.

Next day, after reaching Tofoa, Bligh made an entry in the rescued log of the *Bounty*. "I had scarce got a furlong on my way when I began to reflect on the vicissitudes of human affairs; but in the midst of all I felt an inward happiness which prevented any depression of my spirits, conscious of my own integrity and anxious solicitude for the good of the Service I was on. I found my mind most wonderfully Supported and began to conceive hopes notwithstanding so heavy a Calamity, to be able to recount to my King and country my misfortune." Yes, indeed. How was he to account for the loss of the *Bounty* when he got home? If he got home.

Already, he was thinking up excuses. Why had the men mutinied, led by an officer? Certainly not due to any fault of Lieutenant Bligh. "It will very naturally be asked," he wrote later, "what could be the reason for such a revolt? In answer to which I can only conjecture, that the mutineers flattered themselves with the hopes of a more happy life among the Otaheiteans, than they could possibly enjoy in England; and this, joined to some female connexions, most probably occasioned the whole transaction." No one was to be allowed to think that the crew might have mutinied because they preferred life in Tahiti to life in the *Bounty* under

Bligh; no, Bligh blandly suggests that they preferred life in Tahiti to life in *England*.

A truer picture of the "female connexions" can be found in Fryer's narrative: "I can only say that Christian was not particularly attached to any Woman at Otaheite; nor any of them, except Mr. Stewart and James Morrison, Boatswain's Mate—who were the only two that had there particular Girls. So from what they said I suppose that they did not like their Captain." Which was the understatement of the century.

Why had the mutiny succeeded? Again, Bligh reasoned that he was in no way to blame. It had been too secret and too well planned. Even the seamen knew nothing about it. "The secrecy of this mutiny is beyond all conception . . . the thirteen of the party who came with me and lived allways forward among the people . . . could not discover some symptoms of bad intentions among them. This mutiny has however been long planned, if I may with propriety take the cutting of the cable as a beginning, altho at the time I thought it was done by the Indians. . . . With such deep laid plans of villany and my mind free of any suspicions it is not wonderful that I have been got the better of." No, certainly no one could blame Bligh. He could face the inevitable court martial, for the loss of his ship, with confidence. But could he?

There was one awkward fact—Christian had taken the ship with no more than eight or ten men. Fewer than a quarter of the ship's company, much fewer. And no one had made an actual physical attempt to resist the mutineers and retake the *Bounty,* in spite of the fact that they had all been milling about together for more than three hours, while they quarreled about the boats, and who was to go in them, and with what (which by no means argued for a carefully planned mutiny). Indeed, there had been no casualties whatever, on either side, not even a black eye. The nearest thing to an assault had been the waving of a bayonet in Bligh's face.

If Bligh was to be acquitted, it was necessary for him to have been outnumbered; for a handful of loyalists to have been overpowered by an overwhelming force of mutineers. By constant argument in the boat, Bligh managed to convince himself—and the two miserable midshipmen, Hayward and Hallet—that this had indeed been so. They discussed who had been concerned in the mutiny, and by attributing a black look to one, and a sullen countenance to another, and at the same time, by interpreting an expression of joy as a sign that still another was delighted by the turn of events—they eventually managed to include almost everyone remaining in the ship among the mutineers, even the gardener, William Brown, and some men who had been kept below and who had never even been seen. There were nineteen men in the launch, and more than two dozen still in the *Bounty;* that did not look good, but it was beginning to look better, much better. Within hours of having given it, Bligh forgot his promise to the men who had been detained aboard by Christian's orders, and also to the men whom he himself had ordered not to come into the boat with him, because it was already overloaded. His cry, "I'll do you justice, lads, I know who's who," was to be a promise most bitterly dishonoured.

After spending a night in the boat—it was very cramped, and few got much sleep—they came close in to the heavy surf beating on the shore at Tofoa. Only those who could swim were able to go ashore and search for water and breadfruit. Fryer was a typical old-time British seaman, admitting frankly, "For my part I should have made but little progress in the water as I never could learn to swim." Surprisingly, one of those who could was Mr. Samuel and, for his pains, Bligh ordered him to brave the surf and explore the possibilities of the island. Bligh, like Fryer, remained in the boat. According to Fryer, there was a good deal of bad feeling; naturally enough. Although Bligh would be able to represent that the eighteen other men in the boat with him were his loyal supporters, this was not so. He had only one, Mr. Samuel. The rest were not loyal to Bligh, but to the Navy; and, besides, they had not wanted to risk—with Bligh, it was virtually a certainty—the charge of piracy, by remaining in the safety of the ship. They all regarded Bligh as the author of their misfortunes which, some feared, might prove fatal.

Somebody mentioned that it was Cole who had got them the launch instead of the small, leaky jolly boat. Bligh asked Cole if there was any truth in that, and Cole replied: "Yes, you would never have got the launch yourself."

Even the quiet, self-effacing botanist, Mr. Nelson—whom Bligh tried to use as his confidant—was quite sure where the root of the trouble lay. "Never mind, Mr. Nelson," said Fryer once, "have a good heart, we shall see old England and tell them our grievances by and by."

"Aye, Mr. Fryer, Sir Joseph Banks will ask me a number of questions—be assured that I will speak the truth if ever I live to see him."

But Nelson did not survive to tell his story. Fryer himself—as he makes clear, while at the same time covering his tracks carefully—was by now a bitter opponent of Bligh; and he was backed by Cole and Purcell, also old seamen of the same stamp as himself—rigid, conservative, tradition bound, unable to criticise their superiors except by insinuations which would be understood in the right quarters. However, the ranks were soon to be closed by the threat of danger, for Tofoa, although one of the Friendly Isles, was anything but friendly to the virtually defenceless.

They spent several days at Tofoa, finding at first only a few natives who could not supply them with much food; then, as more and more natives arrived by canoe, the situation became ugly. They began putting stones in their canoes—Bligh was surprised at the power with which they could throw them—and one man came off and swam round the boat. He was probably a diver, for Fryer says that he swam away, as if to leave them, and then suddenly reappeared, grasped the stem of the boat with one hand to haul himself up, and removed a blanket from it with the other. Fryer took hold of an oar and jabbed at him, and he let go the blanket.

It was now nearly sunset. Bligh was on shore, talking to the natives, who were trying to trap him into spending the night on the beach; when he refused, saying he always slept in his boat, they began to knock stones together. This, as Bligh knew, was the preparatory signal for attack. He then walked down the beach, with, as he wrote, "everyone in a silent kind of horror."

As he saw his captain coming down the beach, Fryer had the boat hauled in on the rope, until she grounded stern-first in the surf, ready to take him off. Immediately, a group of natives rushed forward, took hold of the rope, and began to haul hard on it in order to get the boat firmly and irrevocably aground. Fryer at once ordered the boat end of the rope to be slackened. The result was that the natives, tugging hard at the rope, and suddenly being given a lot more of it, fell over backwards in a heap. Bligh called out, "Mr. Fryer, let the boat come on shore."

"Sir, she is on shore, and if she beat she will fill with water," shouted Fryer, whose knowledge of boat handling in a surf was at least equal to Bligh's. "You must come into the water, and I will haul you in."

Purcell, the irascable old carpenter, was on the beach with Bligh; and he stuck grimly to his captain in the rapidly worsening situation. The natives were still trying to haul the boat up, and being frustrated by Fryer. Every time they hauled, he abruptly gave them some slack; and as they staggered or fell, he quickly hauled in again. "Come into the boat, Mr. Bligh," he roared, "or she'll knock her bottom out!" The heavily-laden craft was lurching dangerously in the disturbed water where the waves were breaking on the beach. A hail of stones came suddenly from the natives, and Bligh and Purcell went dashing into the surf, wading out against the waves. With Fryer hauling, and Purcell pushing, Bligh went into the boat with a rush. Simultaneously, one of the quartermasters, John Norton—the man who had dropped the pork overboard—jumped out of the boat and, with desperate bravery, ran up the beach to cast off the grapnel rope. This was not the boat rope, at which the natives were tugging, but another rope attached to a grapnel, which held her to the beach. Fryer, still trying to get Bligh into the boat, called Norton to come back. But he ran on, and the natives were onto him in an instant. He stayed, a moment, struggling, and then went down. The men in the boat could see the stones in the natives' hands rising and falling, as they battered him to pulp. No attempt was made to rescue him.

Bligh, soaked to the skin, fell into the bottom of the boat; and with Purcell still in the water, hanging on to the stern, they tried to fend off from the beach with the oars. The natives were still pulling on the boat rope, trying to haul them in, and Bligh promptly cut it with a knife. In trying to manoeuvre away by hauling on the grapnel rope, it got foul of the coral, and held them to the spot; then one of the grapnel's flukes broke. In indescribable confusion—for the boat was crowded and rolling heavily in the high surf—they unshipped the oars and, with Fryer steering, pulled off with painful slowness. They could see the natives launching their canoes and higher up the beach, five of them crowded round the body of John Norton. Two of them were still beating at the wretched man with stones.

One of Bligh's relatives, the Reverend James Bligh, afterwards wrote: "I have heard Captain Bligh say it was, with respect to the boat's crew, a fortunate circumstance, for he (Norton) was the stoutest man in the ship, which circumstance would very materially have interfered with the boat's progress and the allowance of provisions."

It was true, the boat was now higher in the water. But it

was still slow and lumbering. The light native canoes, loaded with stones for ammunition, came rapidly down upon them. Soon, blood was streaming down the face of Mr. Peckover, the gunner, and several other men had been hurt. The crew of the boat could make no reply, except by hurling back the few stones which lodged in the boat; and they discovered at once that their throws, in accuracy and power, did not compare with those of the natives.

Bligh and the botanist, Mr. Nelson, then threw overboard some clothes and the provisions they had bought, at such cost, from the natives of Tofoa. The canoes stopped repeatedly, while the natives leapt overboard and collected the articles and the boat was able to increase its distance from them. Night was coming on, and a heavy sea was beginning to run; with relief, the men in the boat saw the canoes abandon the chase and go back to Tofoa.

The foremast was erected, and as the sail filled, they began to discuss what to do. Bligh wanted to keep the provisions already in the boat as a reserve; to obtain enough for their immediate wants from a nearby island, which Fryer called Tongataboo. Cole objected. "We shall be treated the same there as we have been at Tofoa."

"Oh no," said Bligh, "they are a different kind of people."

Fryer thought a while, and then said: "Pray, sir, had you any words with the natives of Tongataboo when you was there with Captain Cook?"

"Yes, we had several of them in confinement for theft."

"If that is the case, sir, then they will play us some trick."

"Well then, Mr. Fryer," said Bligh, irritably, "what is the best to be done?"

Fryer then suggested that, instead of working to windward as they were doing, in search of a really friendly Friendly Island, they should put the helm up and go before the wind, thus covering a much greater distance in the time, with the possibility of finding more hospitable shores. Cole grunted his assent. "I'd sooner trust to providence and live on an ounce of bread than go to Tongataboo. If we get there, the natives will take everything from us, even if they don't cut us all to pieces." There was a murmur of agreement.

Bligh was already half-convinced. The natives were friendly, he suspected, only when Europeans were equipped with firearms.

They then began to work out how long their provisions would last. They estimated that the bread would last six weeks, if they rationed each man to one ounce a day; the water would last three weeks at a quarter of a pint per man per day. That was all very well now, but the onset of thirst and hunger might make them change their minds; and it was a discredited Bligh who had to command them. Finally, he said, "Are you all agreeable to live on an ounce of bread and a gill of water per day?" There were cheerful shouts of, "Yes, sir!" They were glad that something had been decided, at any rate. But Bligh made them promise, solemnly, that they would stick to this agreement, no matter what happened. "Shall I put the helm up, sir?" hinted Fryer.

"For God's sake, yes," said Bligh. The launch wallowed round and, putting her stern to the wind and sea, began to lurch westward through the waves at a comforting speed, but with water continually coming inboard.

There was still the question of exactly where to head for on a course which must be westerly because of the prevailing wind. Peckover, the gunner, suggested Timor—he had seen the Dutch settlement on that island when passing through the Straits of New Holland with Captain Cook. Fryer was bitter with Bligh and Samuel for thinking so much about "there Books" (the log and other documents), while what he privately considered to be the real seaman had been seeing to the essentials, such as oars and sails. As it happened, the only really useful book to be brought away from the *Bounty* was in the kit of midshipman Hallet. This was the standard textbook on navigation, which included the tables used for determining latitude and longitude. The book showed them that Timor lay a little to the north of Endeavour Straits. They had a compass, a sextant, and a quadrant, so the navigation was easy. Fryer could certainly have done it, and probably some of the others could have, too. The real problems were: the actual boat handling; and the question of survival.

They were faced by three killers: the sea, the sun, and the wind. And in their battle with the elements, they were to be weakened and tormented by thirst and hunger. The sea came first.

At daybreak, they were alone, a speck on a wide, wide sea, totally enclosed by the waves riding on before the gale; in the east, the sky was red and fiery, sure sign of more wind to come. As the wind rose, the waves became increasingly huge and steep; in their troughs, the sail was totally becalmed, but when the lumbering boat lurched over the crests, the wind screamed and tore wildly at it, so that the launch moved erratically in fits and starts, bows veering dangerously. Cole, the boatswain, was steering now, having taken over from Fryer; it was fortunate that there were aboard it so many experienced, middle-aged seamen, for there were much worse trials to come. They preferred to keep Bligh away from the helm, since his special skill was not the handling of small boats; it was hydrography. Nevertheless, Bligh's book on the voyage was to provoke from Fryer the justified comment, "Captain Bligh has not mentioned any body's services but his own." This type of deliberate omission occurred again many years later when Bligh was in at the "kill" of a Dutch flagship, and somehow forgot to mention the three or four other ships which had been hammering her to splinters hours before he came alongside. But on the launch he did not lack courage, and calmly continued to write up the log, make natural history and navigational observations, and even catalogue a group of islands which had not been on the map before.

All day, they had to bail; and as the bread was in danger of being spoilt, Bligh had the carpenter's tools taken out of the chest and laid in the bottom of the boat; into the chest, which was reasonably watertight, went the bread. Then he examined everybody's personal kit, and ditched everything which was not essential, thus lightening the boat somewhat, and enabling the bailers to get at the water sloshing about in the bottom. Dinner that day consisted of a quarter of a bread-fruit and a teaspoonful of rum (for they were all soaked to the skin and shivering in the strong wind). Bligh, pursetight as ever—but with more justification now—was determined that the provisions should be issued in minute quantities in order to last a period of eight weeks. It was a pessimistic estimate, and unduly weakened them all, prematurely; but it pleased Bligh, gave him the feel of being in command again, of having responsibility laid on his shoulders. It was certainly a factor in his own personal survival.

Bligh altered course slightly, to take him past where he believed, from what he had been told, the Fiji Islands lay. By sailing from one group of islands to the next, he would have a check on his navigation—although he does not say this. When the gale blew itself out, he had a length of rope marked out as a log line, so that they could get some idea of their speed and of the distance run—another check on navigation. By now—it was May 7—they were among a chain of islands which rose up, jagged and fantastic, from the sea. Perched on the high volcanic peaks were native sentinels, scanning the waters in search of prey, which their swift canoes could go out to attack. A hundred eyes saw the *Bounty's* launch come sailing in among the islands; to them, a strange, European craft, an unknown quantity. Easy booty, and white meat for the bamboo knives and stone ovens? Or a murderous musket volley that would make many women widows? Two sailing canoes were launched, to find out.

Bligh's men, gazing with longing at the green groves ashore, fertile with breadfruit, coconuts, bananas, and at the cooling streams cascading over volcanic rocks down to the sea, saw the native sails following in pursuit. There was no landing here, without muskets. The canoes might mean life, but they suspected that they meant death. The oars were unshipped and, Bligh steering, the launch began to cream heavily through the still, calm, blue sea. By afternoon, one of the canoes had obviously gained on them—it was now two miles away. The other was still in the same relative position as it had been when they first sighted it. Bligh's insistence on taking the helm at this critical juncture was much resented by the experienced seamen aboard; Cole, the boatswain, and Elphinstone, the master's mate, in particular, found fault with Bligh's steering. Their alarm increased, as the Fiji war canoe came down upon them, gaining rapidly. "Heave away, lads," shouted Bligh, "if they come up with us, they will cut us all to pieces." There was a snort from old Lawrence Lebogue, the sailmaker. "Damn my eyes, sir, you frighten us all out of our wits. Let the thieves come, and be damned; we will fight as long as we can." Then he began to mutter to himself, "Very pretty indeed, by God, that the captain is the first man frightened." Fryer had to shut him up. It is to be doubted if Bligh was any more frightened than the rest; but his normal excitable manner was specially likely to irritate the others when a battle was in prospect, and every man liked to be quiet and thoughtful. No doubt he thought he was encouraging them; it was not the first time he had struck a wrong note.

Soon afterwards, the pursuing canoe gave up the chase—perhaps it was getting too far from home; perhaps its crew were perturbed by the idea of going alone into battle against a possibly superior opponent, for the launch was crowded with men, more men than the canoe held. It was indeed a Fiji canoe, but the islands were known for some time afterwards as Bligh's Islands, before reverting to their original native name. Bligh coolly charted them as he went past, an accurate chart which later surveys confirmed.

Day after day, the launch bore on westwards. When rain came, they caught some of it, which eased their thirst, but at the same time they were left soaked, shivering, and cramped. There was never room enough in the boat for them all to lie down and get a proper sleep; starvation and loss of sleep rendered the cold almost unendurable. It seemed they would never again be warm. And yet, they were fortunate; it was better than the sun; the sun would have turned them into dehydrated husks within days. To avoid quarrels over the rations, Bligh made a pair of scales out of coconut shells; the weights were pistol balls. To keep out the worst of the stern sea, a canvas weather cloth was fitted round the boat, raising the after part a further nine inches above the waves. Rain and gale was their portion, with occasionally a few hours of sunshine, when they could try to dry out their constantly wet clothing. They suffered from stomach pains and, from lack of exercise, had partially lost the use of their limbs. On May 20, Bligh had to write: "At dawn of day, some of my people seemed half dead: our appearances were horrible; and I could look no way, but I caught the eye of some one in distress. Extreme hunger was now too evident, but no one suffered from thirst, nor had we much inclination to drink, that desire, perhaps, being satisfied through the skin. The little sleep we got was in the midst of water."

The night of May 22 was one of horror; a heavy gale that kept them bailing without a break, threatening continually to overwhelm their sluggish unseaworthy craft. Several of the men seemed to be almost gone. But they recovered two days later, when the sun burst through onto the lonely boat struggling across the great ocean. Bligh immediately decided to reduce the rations still further, in case he missed Timor and had to go on to Java. This was a mistake, but, the reasons having been explained, the men "cheerfully agreed."

On May 25 they caught a noddy, a bird about the size of a small pigeon. The bird, with its entrails, was divided into eighteen portions—by no means equal. The portions were laid out, and one man turned his back to them. Another man then pointed to a particular portion, calling out, "Who shall have this?" The man with his back to the portions then named somebody at random. This was the method, traditional at sea, which the crew of the *Bounty* had used—it seemed so long ago now—when Bligh had kept them on short rations in the ship. Now, the wheel had turned—and Lieutenant Bligh had to take his chance with the rest for a portion of breast or a bit of beak or entrail. That evening, they caught a booby, a bird as large as a duck, which made a better ration for eighteen starving men. The blood was given to three men who seemed far gone.

The night of May 28 was very dark. Fryer was on watch, an hour after midnight, when he heard a curious noise; it sounded like the bursting of waves on distant rocks. The helmsman thought he heard it, too, and Fryer stood up, peering into the dark. At length, he was able to see the breakers—in a dangerous position for the boat, the wind blowing them down onto the rocks. But by lowering the sail, and then rowing, the men kept their distance until the morning, when Fryer spotted a hole in the reef. They glided through it and came to anchor in a patch of marvellously smooth water. For the first time in four weeks, the boat was not in violent motion. They were inside a coral reef protecting a group of small islands, barren and apparently uninhabited. Consequently, they decided to land and, as the boat grounded in the shallows, they got out and began to stagger about the beach like drunken men, cramped and light-headed.

Once ashore, they found oysters and began to collect them

from various parts of the island. Fryer, returning with one of these parties to the boat, asked Cole and Peckover how they had fared. They answered that "Bligh was in sad passion, calling Every Body the Name that he could think of, telling them that if it had not been for him that they would not have been there." Then Nelson, the peace-loving botanist, broke in violently, "Yes, damn his blood, it is his Oeconomy that brought us here."

They stayed there for several days, during which, wrote Fryer, "Captain Bligh did nothing but make a great Noise and write his remarks. The last day, he was sitting under a tree almost all day, writing. I thought that Captain Bligh had been taking off the Land and the adjacent Isles, but Mr. Hallet told me that he was correcting the prayer Book—after we sailed from this Isle we had a new prayer night and morning."

On the last day of May, they again landed on another island to collect oysters. Under the stress of privation, tempers finally broke down. Fryer told Bligh that some of the men had been idle in collecting oysters before, and that there ought to be some relationship between what work a man did and what he ate. Bligh agreed. Elphinstone butted in, saying that he would rather stay in the boat than go after oysters. Fryer agreed that an exception should be made for those who were sick. They then divided up into three parties, found plenty of oysters, and began to return to the boat.

As Fryer approached, he heard Bligh arguing with Purcell, the carpenter, who had been the first to fill his bag with oysters. Bligh was pouring a torrent of abuse on his head.

"You damn scoundrel," he was yelling. "What have I brought you here for! If I hadn't been with you, you would all have perished!"

"Yes, sir, if it hadn't been for you, sir, we should not have been here," said the carpenter pointedly.

"What's that you say, sir!"

"I say, sir, if it had not been for you we should not have been here."

"You damned scoundrel, what do you mean?"

"I am not a scoundrel, sir," said the enraged warrant officer, "I am as good a man as you in that respect."

Up to now, Bligh had only waved his arms. Now, he drew a cutlass and began to brandish it wildly over Purcell's head. Purcell thought Bligh was going to kill him, and said so. Bligh told him to get another cutlass and defend himself. For a moment, it looked as if there was to be a ludicrous, yet possibly tragic, duel. Then Fryer stepped forward.

"I put you both under arrest," he said.

Bligh whirled on him. "By God, sir, if you offered to touch me I would cut you down!"

"Sir, this is not the time to talk of fighting."

"That man," spluttered Bligh, pointing to Purcell. "That man told me he was as good a man as I am!"

"When you called me a scoundrel, I told you I was not," protested the carpenter, "but as good a man as you in *that* respect."

The uproar, according to Bligh, lasted a quarter of an hour; then it died away, probably from the general weakness and unsteadiness of the participants, into minor wrangles. Afterwards, Bligh called Fryer over to one side, out of earshot of the others. It was probably the only time he ever abused an officer in private. "Mr. Fryer," he hissed. "Your behaviour has been most improper. If you ever again interfere with me while I am in the execution of my duty, and should any future tumult arise, I shall certainly put you to death, the first person." For the first time in his life, Bligh probably meant exactly what he said, without exaggeration or passionate embroidery.

"I am very sorry, sir," said Fryer. "But in what way have I behaved improperly?"

"In coming into the boat and saying you would put me under arrest," snapped Bligh.

ROYALTY-THEATRE,
Well-Street, near Goodman's-Fields.

This present THURSDAY, May 6, 1790,
WILL BE PRESENTED
A NEW MUSICAL PIECE, called

TAR against PERFUME:
Or, The SAILOR PREFERRED.

Coxswain, Mr. MATHEWS. William, Mr. BIRKETT. Old Slop, Mr. REES.
And Monsieur Le Friz, (the Perfumer,) Mr. WEWITZER.
Susan, Miss WILLIAMS.

A NEW DANCE, composed by Mr. BOURKE, called
THE MERRY BLOCK-MAKERS.
By Monf. FERRERE, Mad. FOUZZI, Mad FERRERE, Mr. JEANI, Mr. BOURKE, &c.

A MUSICAL ENTERTAINMENT, called
A PILL FOR THE DOCTOR:
Or, The TRIPLE WEDDING.

Sailor, Mr. BIRKETT. Dr Lotion, Mr. REES. Farmer, Mr. MATHEWS.
And Pestle, the Doctor's Man, Mr. WEWITZER.
Polly, Miss WILLIAMS. Dorothy, Mrs. SAUNDERS.
Lydia, Miss E. WILLIAMS. And Goody, Mrs. BURNETT.
To conclude with a DANCE by the Characters.

A FAVOURITE SONG, by Miss DANIEL.

The Whole to conclude with (the 4th Time) A FACT, TOLD IN ACTION, called
The PIRATES:
OR,
The Calamities of Capt. BLIGH.

Exhibiting a full Account of his Voyage, from his taking Leave at the Admiralty.
AND SHEWING,
The BOUNTY falling down the River THAMES.
The Captain's Reception at OTAHEITE, and exchanging the *British Manufactures* for the BREAD-FRUIT TREES. With an OTAHEITEAN DANCE.
The Attachment of the OTAHEITEAN WOMEN to, and their Distress at parting from, the BRITISH SAILORS.
An exact Representation of
The SEISURE of Capt. BLIGH, in the Cabin of the BOUNTY, by the Pirates.
With the affecting Scene of forcing the Captain and his faithful Followers into the Boat.
Their Distress at Sea, and Repulse by the Natives of One of the *Friendly Islands*.
Their miraculous Arrival at the *Cape of Good Hope*, and their friendly Reception by the Governor.
DANCES and CEREMONIES of the HOTTENTOTS
On their Departure. And their happy Arrival in England.
Rehearsed under the immediate Instruction of a Person who was on-board the Bounty, Store-Ship.

_ The Doors to be opened at Half past Five and to begin at Half past Six o'Clock precisely.
BOXES, 3s. 6d.—PIT, 2s. 6d.—FIRST GALLERY, 1s. 6d.—UPPER GALLERY, 1s.
Nothing under full Price will be taken nor any Money returned:
Places for the Boxes may be taken at the Stage-Door from Ten till Three o'Clock every Day.
VIVANT REX & REGINA.

☞ BOOKS of the PILL for the DOCTOR to be had at the Theatre; and, to prevent Imposition, the Proprietors have ordered that no more shall be taken for them than SIX-PENCE each.

FACSIMILE OF A PLAY-BILL
In the possession of Charles H. Bertie Esq

'The Calamities of Capt. Bligh' on the contemporary stage, 1790. Facsimile of a playbill. *Photo: from an old print*

George Hamilton, surgeon of HMS *Pandora*, frigate, who kept a diary. *Photo: from an old print*

The wrecked Pandora sinking on the Great Barrier Reef of Australia, 1791. The picture is from a sketch by Peter Heywood, one of the 94 survivors. The wreck was discovered by two Australian divers in 1977 and is being excavated by the Queensland Museum, Brisbane. *Photo: National Maritime Museum, Greenwich*

But Fryer, too, was in earnest. "Sir, will you give me leave to tell you how far I think you was wrong?"

"Me wrong, sir!"

"Yes, sir, you were wrong," said Fryer quietly. "You put yourself on a footing with the carpenter when you took up a cutlass and told him to take another. If he had done so and cut you down, it is my opinion that he would have been justifiable in so doing."

Bligh snorted.

"There are other methods in making people do as they are ordered, without fighting them, sir. And you may rest assured that I will support you in that as far as lays in my power." Awkwardly, the master, very inarticulate, but with the traditions of the service ingrained in him, from an experience much greater than Bligh's, tried to be tactful. The smell of oysters cooking brought the discussion to an end.

Bligh afterwards labelled Fryer "a mean and ignorant fellow, ever disposed to be troublesome and then ready to beg pardon." His own conduct that day, however, he thought brave in the extreme, writing of the sightly absurd cutlass episode: "I, therefore, determined to strike a final blow at it and either to preserve my command or die in the attempt." But he no longer had a command, merely a group of half-starved, quarrelling men.

So far gone were they with privation, that Bligh's purse-tight policy with the rations was creating a vicious circle; some of the men were becoming so weak from starvation that they were unable to search for food on the chain of small, uninhabited islands they were now passing. Next day, June 1, Nelson, the botanist, struggled ashore with one of the search parties; but he had to be carried back by Fryer and Peckover, doubled up with agony in the stomach, half-blind, and unable to walk. Fryer and Peckover were not so very much better off. Fryer was shivering with cold and, as it was getting dark, made a small fire to warm himself. Unfortunately, the sparks set fire to some dry grass nearby, and in a few minutes there was quite a blaze; this brought Bligh running to the spot, swearing that it would give them away to the natives. After midnight, a party sent out to catch turtle returned to report no success. "This did not surprise me," wrote Bligh, "as it was not to be expected the turtle would come near us, after the noise which had been made at the beginning of the evening in extinguishing the fire." Fryer's retort to Bligh was "I do not recollect any Body making a noise but Himself."

A few days later, they were again in the open sea, out of sight of land. They began to see water-snakes, ringed yellow and black, and to suffer once more from thirst. The appropriate passage from *The Ancient Mariner* matches Bligh's log fairly exactly:

> "Water, water, every where,
> And all the boards did shrink;
> Water, water, every where,
> Nor any drop to drink.
>
> The very deep did rot; O Christ!
> That ever this should be!
> Yea, slimy things did crawl with legs
> Upon the slimy sea.
>
> And every tongue, through utter drought,
> Was withered at the root;
> We could not speak . . ."

On June 10, wrote Bligh, "In the morning, after a very comfortless night, there was a visible alteration for the worse in many of the people; Lawrence Lebogue and the surgeon cannot live a week longer if I do not get relief. An extreme weakness, swell'd legs, hollow and gastly countenances, great propensity to sleep, and an apparent debility of understanding, give me melancholy proofs of an approaching disolution of some of my people, if I cannot get to land in the course of a few days." None of them cursed Christian; but some still had the strength to argue with Bligh when, three days later, they reached the neighbourhood of Timor and Bligh failed to recognise it. His excuse, later, was that "the weather was so hazy." Fryer thought the land to be islands some leagues from Timor, Peckover correctly identified one island as Roti. But Bligh set off in the wrong direction, away from Timor and the help they so badly needed. The dispute concluded with Bligh sneering at Fryer "Sir, I suppose you will take the boat from me."

"No, sir. I despise your ideas, but it is far from my intention to take the boat from you."

Bligh answered by threatening to cut Fryer in pieces. Fryer suggests in his book that Bligh was trying to provoke him to a statement "that he could take hold of."

Later in the day, they went ashore and found out the direction in which the Dutch settlement lay, by asking the natives. They anchored for the night and, on the morning of June 14, began to row. Soon after daylight, they saw a small fort and the town of Coupang, with European ships at anchor. Bligh then raised a small Union Jack, which they had made out of signal flags, and the boat with its load of haggard, bearded, emaciated men, entered the harbour and grounded on the beach.

One of Bligh's first actions ashore was to break the bad news to his wife, "Know then, my own dear Betsy, I have lost the *Bounty*." He went on to add, "My own conduct has been free of blame . . . tell them all that they will find my character respectable and honour untarnished." It is clear what was foremost in his mind, but he found time to give the detail, "I have saved my Pursery books so that all my profits hitherto will take place and all will be well." And elsewhere he "cursed the day" he had ever met a Christian or a Heywood or a Manxman. Later on his journey home he wrote his long Despatch to the Admiralty which was in effect a detailed defence of his actions prior to and during the mutiny. Attached to this Despatch was a copy of a "Descriptive List of the Pirates remaining on board His Majesty's Armed Vessel *Bounty* on the 28th April 1789."

They were: Fletcher Christian, who had immediately taken over Bligh's cabin for his own use; three midshipmen, George Stewart, Peter Heywood, and Edward Young; the ship's corporal, Charles Churchill; the armourer, Joseph Coleman; the boatswain's mate, James Morrison; the gunner's mate, John Mills; two carpenter's mates, Charles Norman and Thomas McIntosh; the botanist's assistant, William Brown; and no less than fourteen able seamen—for only four had gone with Bligh in the boat. These seamen were: Thomas Burkett, John Sumner, John Williams, Matthew Thompson, Thomas Ellison, William M'Coy, John Millward, Richard Skinner (ship's barber and master's servant), Matthew Quintal, Michael Byrn (fiddler and boatkeeper), Henry Hillbrant (cooper), Isaac Martin, John Adams (alias Alexander Smith), and William Muspratt (tailor and commander's steward).

Against the names of Coleman, Norman, and McIntosh, Bligh made a note: "These were kept against their consent and are deserving Mercy." The use of the word "Mercy" instead of, perhaps, "Justice" is an interesting sidelight on Bligh's inflamed state of mind. But he was good enough to add also, "Michael Byrn I was told has no knowledge of what was doing." The point at issue was, of course—the more mutineers there were, the better it looked for Bligh. And Bligh with a willing hand was ready to condemn them all.

9
Captain Christian

THE *Bounty* was now a pirate ship. In no civilised port would she be given help. Her only hope was to find a refuge somewhere in the vast, unexplored expanses of the South Seas. The problem of what to do and where to go—simultaneously facing Bligh and his companions—also faced Christian and those with him. And, like those who had gone away in the launch, they were divided in their allegiance. Among the twenty-five men remaining in the *Bounty* there were three different parties—the hard-core mutineers; those who had wanted to accompany Bligh but had been prevented from doing so; and others who, according to Morrison, "hardly knew what part they had acted in the business."

There were eight or ten hard-core mutineers—but three of these had been uncertain. Both Quintal and Martin had wavered at some point during the proceedings and even Millward, who had been flogged for his part in the desertion led by Churchill at Tahiti, had changed his mind several times, saying to Churchill: "No, Charles, you brought me into one predicament already, and I'll take care you don't bring me into another."

Of the three midshipmen, two—Heywood and Stewart—were kept below hatches during the greater part of time by the armed sentinels placed on the gangways. The third—

Edward Young—is an enigma; where he was and what he was doing, no one knows. But if he had been prominent in the mutiny, it would have been observed; like many others, he was probably just a confused spectator. On the other hand, it was Stewart who had touched off the mutiny by suggesting to Christian that, instead of merely deserting, he could take the ship, as the people were "ripe for anything." That he did in fact suggest this is beyond doubt, for one of the first things Christian did, after having got rid of Bligh, was to explain to everyone the real facts of the case; how it had all happened so quickly. Four men had assisted him to desert: Cole, the boatswain; Purcell, the carpenter; and two midshipmen, Stewart and Hayward. But when it came to mutiny, Cole, Purcell, and Hayward had gone with Bligh; only Stewart had remained. Christian's account was repeated, quite independently, by two witnesses—Morrison and John Adams. At the time they made their statements, neither knew what had happened to the other, or even whether he had survived to say anything at all. And although the statements were separated in time by a lapse of some twenty years, they still tallied.

But Stewart, too, had drawn back at the last moment, and wanted to go in the boat; indeed, he had convinced Heywood that it was necessary that they should go, and they had both slipped up on deck. Heywood, seeing how low in the water the launch was, had been most reluctant to risk his life in it; but had finally agreed. While they were below, getting their kit ready, Churchill had settled the matter for them, by ordering the sentry to keep them from returning to the deck.*

The indecision of these two, and also that of some even of the actual mutineers, is hard to understand if they are thought of as mature men, capable of weighing the consequences of their acts. But, in fact, they were all youngsters; for some of

* Heywood later contended that Christian had mistaken Stewart's meaning (Du Rietz, 1965) and was therefore not guilty of taking any part in the mutiny.

them, it was the first time they had ever been to sea. Heywood was seventeen, Stewart twenty-three; most of the able seamen were aged about twenty. It was a collection of kids, led by a young man acting on impulse; hence the muddled nature of the affair. That it succeeded, was a measure of Bligh's incompetence as a manager of men.

Christian, however, although lacking the statutory authority of Bligh, soon had them under control.

He had detained Coleman, because he needed an armourer; Norman and McIntosh, because he needed carpenters; Stewart and Heywood, because he needed officers; and Michael Byrn, because the fiddler was popular on board—the ship's "character". Coleman, Norman, and McIntosh should have been safe—they had called out to Bligh to remember them; Byrn was half-blind, and could hardly be blamed; but the others—even Morrison, who had tried to take part in Fryer's "push"—were in deadly danger, should the ship be retaken. Even the seventeen-year-old Heywood was likely to hang; for Bligh was at this moment busily engaged in totting up as many "mutineers" as he could, and had already convinced himself of Heywood's guilt.

Christian assembled his crew. He had already made up his mind where to go, but he asked them first. Predictably, they shouted for a return to Tahiti. Then, coolly, Christian pointed out the objections. If Bligh's launch reached a European settlement then, sooner or later, Bligh would return to England with his story. A warship, faster and more heavily gunned than the *Bounty,* would be sent out to search for them. Where would it go? Where else but Tahiti? There was a noticeable drop in morale, when that sank in, and then someone asked Christian for his suggestion.

Christian had it ready. They required a little-known island, well out of the track of ships. There was such an island—Tubai, in the Austral group. It was 500 miles from Tahiti, and 1,500 miles from where they were now. It was on Captain

Cook's chart, and was inhabited—but that was the sum total of the available knowledge; they could at least call there, knowing that Tahiti was also available to them if they wanted supplies. The crew agreed. Christian divided them into two watches—with himself in charge of one and Stewart the other—and the *Bounty* wore slowly round onto a south-easterly course, leaving behind her, bobbing on the waves, a long green trail of breadfruit plants. With the last vestige of Bligh's work thrown overboard, to clear cabin space, the *Bounty's* crew settled down under their new master.

Morrison was still entering up his journal and young Peter Heywood was later to write a narrative. Neither of them wished to have any connection with the mutiny, but what were they to do? Morrison got together with Coleman and several others who "were not at all pleased with their situation," but the plot had not even got under way before Christian heard of it. He at once took the keys of the arms chest away from Coleman, moved the arms chest itself into the main cabin, and saw to it that the hard-core mutineers on whom he could rely went about armed with a brace of pistols. Having carried out a successful mutiny himself, he had a pretty good idea of how to stop one. The men he suspected were always watched, and never allowed even to talk to each other without one of his men sauntering up to join them. Before reaching Tubai, he took care to smarten up the ship; new uniforms were made for all hands from sailcloth, edged with the cloth from his own uniform. Nothing, he told them, had more effect on the minds of Indians than uniformity of dress, as it indicated discipline.

They reached Tubai on May 28, and Stewart, in the cutter, led the way in through the reef. He had to fire a warning shot at hostile natives who came out in a canoe. Next morning, the *Bounty* lay at anchor inside the reef, surrounded by canoes, the waters of the lagoon echoing with the blare of conch shells blown by the natives. When Christian went ashore with a landing party, the natives met his friendly overtures with a volley of stones; to which Christian promptly replied with a volley of musket fire. He noted that there were no pigs, no goats, no poultry—a sign that no European ship had ever put in there. He would have to go to Tahiti to get them. As for the natives, the island was small, there could not be many of them; their hostility could be overcome, by persuasion or by force. The *Bounty* sailed from what her crew now referred to as "Bloody Bay." But, as a refuge for mutineers, it had its points—not least, the difficult approach to the anchorage. But it was essential to keep secret his plan to settle there.

Christian therefore ordered that, while at Tahiti, no one was to mention Tubai. He did not intend to have any desertions at Tahiti either, as this also would give away the secret of the settlement. Bligh had had three men flogged for desertion. Anyone who deserted now would not be flogged—he would be shot. There was a growl of assent from the mutineers, whose own lives now hung on the prevention of desertion. Peter Heywood had been planning it, but Christian had thought the matter out. The policy that had served Cook and Bligh would now serve him; if anyone got away, he would force the natives to restore the man. And then he would execute him.

On June 6, the *Bounty* dropped anchor in Matavai Bay. Christian had already distributed the remaining trade goods among his crew; unlike Bligh, he told them that what they did with these articles was their business. He had already coached them in the story they were to tell the Tahitians, to explain the *Bounty's* swift return. Now, as the natives came up delightedly and began to ask where "Brihe" and the others were, Christian replied that they had met Captain Cook, who had taken Bligh and the others with him, and also the breadfruit; he had been sent back with the ship to procure hogs and goats for a new settlement which the King of England was making in New Holland. "Nor do I think they would have thought any worse of us," commented Morrison, "had they known the truth of the Story or been in anyway shy of supplying us, as Mr. Christian was beloved by the whole of them, but on the Contrary none liked Mr. Bligh tho' they flattered him for his Riches, which is the Case among polished Nations, those in power being always Courted."

By June 16, with 460 pigs, 50 goats, and a number of chickens, dogs, and cats aboard, they were ready to sail. Also aboard the *Bounty,* wrote Morrison, were "9 men, 8 boys, 10 weomen, and one female child, some of which hid themselves below till we were at sea." When these natives were told that they would never see Tahiti again, "they seemed perfectly easy and satisfied, never betraying the least sign of sorrow for leaving their friends." There had been no desertions at Tahiti, no executions, and no floggings.

But already Bligh and the seventeen other survivors of the open boat voyage had been forty-eight hours ashore at Coupang. Soon, they were to return to England.

The *Bounty* reached Tubai on June 23. This time the natives, having tasted musketry, were friendly; and the Tahitians were able to act as interpreters. Christian explained that the Europeans and their Tahitian friends wanted to settle on the island, and one of the chiefs agreed to let them build on a piece of land by the shore. Christian warped the *Bounty* into position opposite it, and landed the livestock; then he went to find a site for the fort which would dominate the position. Two of the hard-core mutineers, Quintal and Sumner, then went ashore without permission and did not return until the next day. There was hard work ahead, so Christian dealt decisively with them. First, he asked them why they had landed without his permission. They were surly, and answered: "The ship is moor'd and we are now our own masters."

For answer, Christian drew Bligh's pistol, which he carried always in his pocket, pointed it at them, remarking, "I'll let you know who is master," and had them put in irons. One night in irons was sufficient, and they were released next day.

"Fort George," as Christian named the settlement, was to be a formidable structure 100 yards square and enclosed by a 20-foot ditch; on the thick walls, the guns of the *Bounty* were to be mounted. Leading the work in person, Christian forced the pace; by September 1 the gateposts were up and the walls nearly finished. When Christian talked of using the masts of the *Bounty* in the construction, Peter Heywood thought he saw his chance. Once the ship was rendered incapable of pursuit, it would be safe for a small party to escape in the jolly boat. He discussed the matter with Stewart and Morrison; but the boat's unseaworthy state—it had been considered unfit even for Bligh—was the chief objection. As Morrison wrote, "it was a foolish attempt, as, had we met with bad weather, our crazy boat would certainly have made us a coffin."

Meanwhile, trouble was brewing with the natives, and between Christian and his crew. The natives did not object to the seamen visiting the women in the native huts, when the males were present, but—unlike the Tahitians—they objected most strongly to the Europeans taking the females of their fancy out to the ship. Tubai was proving to be quite the most inhospitable port the crew had ever visited—and this was where they were to spend the rest of their lives. Even Portsmouth—with its army of soiled amazons—was better. A deputation waited upon Christian with the demand that he lead an armed party in order "to get them each a woman to live with." Christian refused, and suggested they try persuasion. So they went on strike: no women, no work. After three days, they again approached him: if they could not have women, they would have drink; they demanded more grog. Knowing the certain consequences, he refused. So they broke open the spirit store, and helped themselves. It was mutiny again.

Christian met it, on September 10, by calling a conference.

He asked them what they wanted to do. There was a babble of contradictory suggestions, then some moved formally that they should return to Tahiti, "and there separate where they might get weomen without force."

"Gentlemen," said Christian, "I will carry you and land you wherever you please. I desire no one to stay with me against his will. I have but one favour to ask: that you will grant me the ship, tie the fore-sail, give me a few gallons of water, and leave me to run before the wind, and I shall land upon the first island she drives to." He paused. "I have done such an act that I cannot stay at Otaheite. I will never live where I may be carried home to be a disgrace to my family."

The answer was immediate. "There are some of us will never leave you," shouted Young. And there was a chorus from half a dozen or more of the others, "Aye, aye, sir, we will stay by you, go where you will."

Christian immediately put the matter to the vote. "For Otaheite?" Sixteen hands were raised. "For the *Bounty*?" Eight hands were raised. Very well then, they would go to Tahiti, and then separate; there would be a fair division of arms, ammunition, and stores. Meanwhile, they had better collect the stock, and get them back on board the ship.

The small party sent out to round up the pigs, goats, and other animals ran into trouble at once. They were attacked by natives, plundered, beaten up, and sent back in disorder to Christian, with a message from the natives that he would be treated in the same way if they caught him. Christian immediately paraded his men, and leaving a small force behind, sent out a party of twenty heavily armed seamen, nine Tahitian men, and four Tahitian boys to gather in the stock. The party was ambushed by a native war party estimated at 700 strong, "armed with clubbs, spears and stones." Now, "Bloody Bay" really earned its name, ringing with war cries, the raw screams of the wounded, and the bang and rattle of musketry and pistol fire, until the natives had had enough. Next day, they attacked again, and Burkett was wounded; again, the natives were repulsed with heavy loss. The Tahitians were delighted, and busied themselves collecting plunder; one of the boys had to be dissuaded from cutting out the jawbones of the dead—he thought that, hung around the sides of the *Bounty,* they would have a marked deterrent effect upon potential enemies. A native chief friendly to Christian now came aboard; he reported that native losses included sixty men dead and six women killed, with very many wounded. They were so incensed that he and his companions, being known friends of the Europeans, could expect no mercy once the *Bounty* left; he begged Christian for a passage for them all to Tahiti. Christian agreed, and when they sailed there were six Tubaian men and twelve Tubaian women aboard the *Bounty*. The discrepancy between the sexes rather suggests that some, at least, of her crew had been trying the recommended policy of persuasion.

The *Bounty* made a fast passage to Tahiti, arriving at Matavai Bay for the last time on September 22. In lighthearted mood, those aboard divided up the stores, the tools, the arms, and the ammunition. The sixteen who had chosen to disembark at Tahiti included seven who had taken no part in the mutiny—the two midshipmen, Heywood and Stewart, who had been kept below by Churchill; the three technicians, Norman, McIntosh, and Coleman, who had been detained by Christian because he needed them; Morrison, who had agreed with Fryer to take part in his "push" to retake the ship; and the half-blind fiddler, Byrn, who had got into the launch and been ordered out of it. They were in no danger—they thought—and looked forward to being taken off by a European ship sooner or later. They failed to consider the danger Bligh was in, if it should ever be realized by the Admiralty how few in number the mutineers really had been. But the shore party also included: Churchill, who had been Christian's right-hand man in the taking and holding of the ship; Thompson, Burkett, Sumner, Hillbrant, Millward, and Ellison, all of whom had either taken part in the mutiny or had behaved in a too openly delighted manner when it had occurred; Norman and Muspratt, who had momentarily taken up arms; and Skinner, who had actually tried to shoot Bligh when he was in the boat. Although not all of them had formed part of the original assault party under Christian they had, once the ship had been taken, acted in a manner certain to ensure them a hanging, if taken by the Royal Navy. But England seemed far away, and they all dispersed to the houses of their native friends, taking their share of the stores.

Now, wrote Morrison, "It being late before evrything was landed, Mr. Christian told us he intended to stay a day or two, and hoped that we would assist him to fill some water, as he intended to cruize for some uninhabited island where he would land his stock (of which the ship was full, together with plants of all the kinds that are common in these islands) and set fire to the ship, and where he hoped to live the remainder of his days without seeing the face of a European but those who were already with him."

This was perfectly true and, as usual, Christian had made his plans well in advance, but keeping the essential details secret. In his cabin he had a copy of Captain Carteret's book on his voyage round the world in the *Swallow,* during which he had discovered an island that suited exactly all Christian's requirements for a refuge. Christian had decided to colonise it. What he did not know, however, was that Carteret had been more than three degrees out in his estimate of its longitude; the island was nearly 200 miles away from the place he said it was.

That evening, Christian went ashore to say goodbye to Heywood and Stewart, who were installed in the house of a chief whose daughter, Peggy, Stewart was later to marry. Next morning, as they walked with him down to the beach, Christian gave them a final piece of advice. "Go off at once to any ship of war that may appear, and give yourself up," he said. "You are both innocent. No harm can come to you, for you took no part in the mutiny." He then repeated his side of that "unfortunate disaster". When Stewart had called him to take over the watch, he was so upset by Bligh's treatment that his brain seemed on fire; when he came on deck, to find Hayward asleep and Hallet still below, the idea of capturing the *Bounty* had first entered his mind. The entire responsibility was his, he declared emphatically; no one, not even his supporters, were to so much as suggest anything else. This was a clear hint to Stewart not to mention the conversation in which he had said that the people "were ready for anything". It is clear, too, that Christian—like the Ancient Mariner—had an albatross round his neck. One thoughtless, impatient act of his had imperilled all his friends.

Having briefed the two midshipmen on what to say, he shook hands, and stepped into the boat. With him aboard the *Bounty* were a number of native men and women, some of them Tahitians, some of them the people he had brought from Tubai. There were five able seamen, all hard-core mutineers: Williams, Martin, Quintal, Adams (alias Smith), and the rough-neck M'Coy. Additionally, there was the midshipman Edward Young and the gardener William Brown, who appear to have played no part in the mutiny at all.

Those ashore had expected the *Bounty* to remain a few days more, but at daybreak the following morning they saw her standing out to sea. Christian did not intend to risk an attempt by some of those ashore to retake the ship, or to allow the men with him second thoughts. The men on Tahiti were looking on the *Bounty* for the last time. Slowly, the white-sailed ship drew away, headed for the uncharted wastes of the Pacific, never to be seen again.

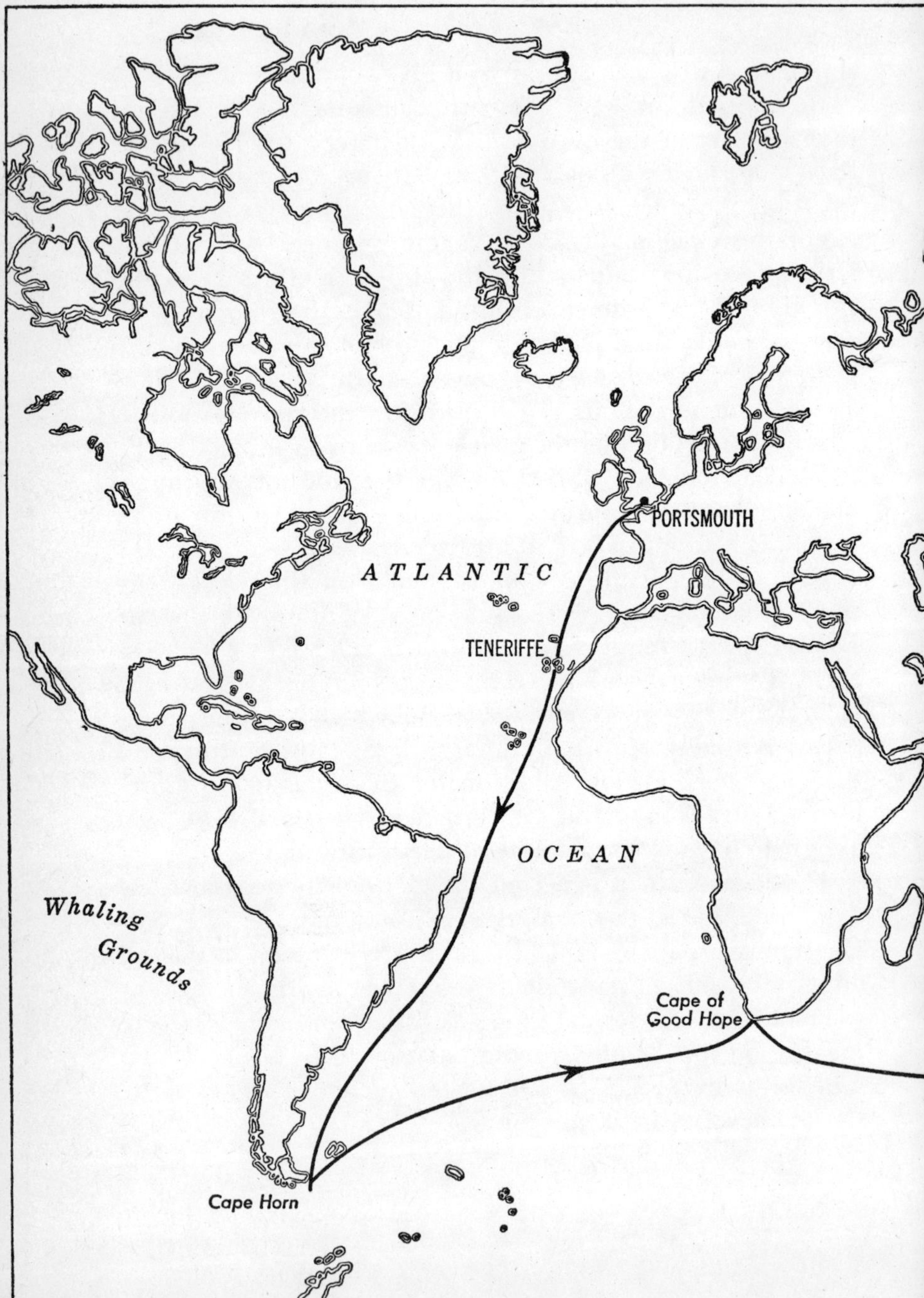

PORTSMOUTH
ATLANTIC
TENERIFFE
OCEAN
Whaling Grounds
Cape of Good Hope
Cape Horn
HAGSTROM CO., N.Y.

PACIFIC
OCEAN
Whaling Grounds
IAN
EAN
COUPANG
TIMOR
Endeavour Straits
TOFOA
TONGA
TAHITI
TUBAI
PITCAIRN
Adventure Bay
LEGEND
BOUNTY under BLIGH
BOUNTY under CHRISTIAN
BLIGH'S BOAT

10
Bligh Writes a "Best Seller"

As the *Bounty* disappeared over the blue horizon, from the sight of the watchers on Tahiti, Bligh was on his way back to England. He was already nearing Batavia, from where he was to send his long Despatch to the Admiralty, and circulate further copies of his "Description List of the Pirates". And he had already had two further mutinies.

When the boat had grounded on the shore at Coupang on June 14, 1789, Bligh had led his ragged castaways ashore; but not all of them. Observing that he had some of his kit in the boat, and that it could not be left, he had sent orders for Fryer and one man to remain with the boat. Both were far gone with privation, and needed medical attention urgently, but, as Fryer remarked, "I might have gone to the Devil for my good friend Captain Bligh." However, a man dressed as a soldier came down to the two haggard men dressed in the rags of uniform, and offered them a "Kettle of Tea and some small cakes". Fryer tried to recollect enough Dutch to tell the man to thank his superiors for their kindness. The reply came in English: "Oh, no I brought them myself. My father is English and I like the English very well. When you come ashore, come to my house." Fryer afterwards wrote, "The man's goodness brought a teer from my eye." At last, after at least three hours, a message arrived for Fryer and the seaman to go to the house of a Captain Spikerman. Fryer first made sure that the order came from Bligh, for he was determined not to give his captain the least excuse for action against him; then, long after the others, he and the seaman went up to join a dinner party which was being prepared by the Dutch Governor for the survivors of what was then the longest voyage ever recorded in an open boat. A number of them, however, weakened by the ordeal, were never to see England again; they died at various points of the long journey home.

They were all, of course, penniless; but they had to be housed and fed, and Bligh wanted to purchase a schooner, the *Resource,* to take them all to England. Bligh pledged the credit of the British Government to cover these necessary expenses, and at first the Dutch Governor accepted without demur; then he asked for the signature of another officer, in addition to Bligh's, as a guarantee of security. Bligh was furious, and in his private journal blamed Fryer, "a viscious person," who had become friendly with Captain Spikerman—"a man much disrespected here," according to Bligh. Captain Spikerman's wife, he thought, must have whispered something to the governor. But what had she whispered? Fryer supplies the answer. Captain Spikerman had given, without question of reward, a house for the accommodation of the survivors; Spikerman himself told Fryer that he did not intend to charge for it. But shortly after, Bligh told Fryer that, he, Bligh, was paying for the hire of the house. The inference was obvious—Bligh was charging up the cost of hiring the house to the Admiralty, and then pocketing the money himself. A neat little racket, recalling Bligh's successful "speculation" at the Cape, and the allegations of his crew that he was "playing the purser" with them as far as the rations were concerned. Whatever the facts of the matter, the net result was that the governor suspected Bligh of being dishonest.

The survivors also needed a certain amount of personal spending money; here the evidence of Bligh's methods comes, not from an enemy of Bligh, but from the acting surgeon, Thomas Denman Ledward. At Spithead, he had written to his uncle: "The captain, though a passionate man, is, I believe, a good hearted man and has behaved very handsomely to me." After landing at Timor, he had written to his uncle of the mutiny: "The sad affair happened early in the morning watch. As soon as I was informed fully how the matter stood, I instantly declared I would go with the captain, let the consequence be that it may, and not stay among the mutineers." But in the last letter he was ever to write to his uncle (for he was lost at sea between Batavia and the Cape) Ledward said: "There is one thing I must mention which is of consequence; the captain denied me, as well as the rest of the gentlemen who had not agents, any money unless I would give him my power attorney and also my will, in which I was to bequeath to him all my property, this he called by the name of proper security. This unless I did, I should have got no money, though I showed him a letter of credit from my uncle and offered to give him a bill of exchange upon him. In case of my death I hope this matter will be clearly pointed out to my Relations."

Did Bligh ever try to cash in on the will? It would be interesting to know. But there is one certainty: the best fiddler in the ship was not Michael Byrn.

The journey home was one long round of recriminations too tedious to recount in full, but one—which occurred at Timor—also had a bearing on Bligh's honesty. Purcell, the carpenter, told Bligh to his face that, during the boat voyage, he had seen him frequently drop a piece of bread, while serving out the rations, and afterwards, when he thought no one was looking, pick it up and pop it in his mouth. Linkletter, one of the quartermasters, backed Purcell up: he, too, had seen Bligh conjuring an extra piece for himself. Bligh retaliated in the customary Service way; within twenty-four hours he had "picked on" Purcell and Linkletter, and had them imprisoned on board Captain Spikerman's ship. That made the rest very wary. But it did not make them love Bligh more; not one shred of respect for him remained. Another explosion was bound to come.

On July 6, he "picked on" Fryer, taking advantage of the fact that the man was ill, and ordering him to supervise Purcell's work as carpenter on the outfitting of the *Resource*. The ball went backwards and forwards for some time, Fryer just about keeping his temper under control and his replies a hair's breadth short of insolence, until Bligh gave up the contest with a final burst of temper: "If you were home now, it would rest with me if you stay'd five minutes in the Service." Fryer replied quietly that he prayed to God they would get home, for the matter would have to be cleared up.

Nelson, the botanist, died on July 20 and was buried at Timor; he was merely the first to perish in consequence of the open boat voyage. A month later, the remainder of Bligh's party sailed in the schooner *Resource,* towing the *Bounty's* launch behind them. She was bound for Batavia, but on the way they put into Sourabaya. Here, on September 16, occurred the affair which Bligh forgot to mention in his published account, but entered in the log under "Particular Transactions at Sourabaya." "Peculiar" would have been a better description: it was virtually a major mutiny. Bligh's and Fryer's narratives, taken together, tell the story.

Bligh had invited the governor of Sourabaya, Anthony Barkay, and the commandant of the troops, M. de Bose, on board the *Resource*. Soon after his Dutch guests had arrived, he decided that someone had stolen a bottle of drink and immediately ordered a search to be made for it. It was found in his own cabin, where Mr. Samuel had put it. Bligh then told Fryer to weigh anchor. Fryer called down to the master's mate, Mr. Elphinstone, who called back that he was taken ill. With him was the midshipman, Hallet. Now, according to Fryer, "Lieut. Bligh came in a great Passion and ask the reason why Mr. Elphinstone was not on deck." From there on, Bligh's account and Fryer's interlock, giving virtually the same dialogue.

"Are they drunk or ill, or what is the matter with them?" snapped Bligh.

"I don't know whether Mr. Elphinstone is sick or drunk," answered Fryer.

"You don't know whether he is sick or drunk?"

"No, sir."

"God damn you, sir, why don't you know?"

"Am I a doctor, sir? Ask him whether they are sick or not."

"What do you mean by this insolence?" raged Bligh, adding a number of words which neither man saw fit to put down on paper afterwards.

"It is no insolence. You not only use me ill, but every man in the vessel, and every man will say the same—"

As usual, Bligh was berating the other officer, his own second in command, in front of a fascinated audience of seamen. But this time, he was to regret it, for there was a roar of approval at Fryer's last words. "Yes, by God, we are used damn ill, nor have we any right to be used so!" shouted someone. With Fryer staring with bitter hatred at his young captain, and the seamen roaring angrily and closing in, Purcell stepped forward to Fryer's aid, and repeated the seamen's protest that they were being ill-used and that it wasn't right. The white-faced Bligh was unable to make himself heard for several minutes, as the seamen shouted detailed accusations at him; or, as he put it, "every body on board made an open tumult." Seizing a bayonet, he screamed at Fryer and Purcell: "Go down below this instant!" They obeyed at once.

During this display of British discipline aboard a Bligh-commanded ship, the Dutch governor and the commandant had tactfully retreated to their boat, and put off. Bligh screamed after them from the rail to come back; but they could not understand his ravings and he sent a boat after them. He had Fryer and Purcell brought up on deck and, as the Dutchmen came over the side, charged the carpenter and master with mutiny and asked M. de Bose to imprison them in the barracks ashore. The Dutch commandant showed no trace of surprise, merely remarking that it was common talk among his men that Bligh's officers and crew had told the town's people that Bligh would be hanged or blown from the mouth of a cannon as soon as he got back to England. For a moment, Bligh was flabbergasted—"alarmed" was the word he used.

Then he began to rage for a culprit to be pointed out to him. M. de Bose had his own coxswain brought on board the *Resource*. On being asked who had made this "disgraceful" statement, the Dutchman said that they all had—indicating the crew generally—but that Purcell had been most vehement. At once, the miserable Hayward, according to Bligh, "shocked at such a degree of infamy, in the guilt of which he was, from the [Dutchman's] account, equally involved with the others, fled into my arms, beseeching me that I would not believe he could be possibly guilty of such infamy and ingratitude, and after shedding a torrent of tears, dared any one to assert he was guilty of any such baseness, or in the least degree privy to it, alleging at the same time that he never, but when he was obliged, had any conversation with anyone on board, for he believed they had not good principals. The honour and integrity of this young man made the wretches about him tremble and having gained my good wishes, his grief subsided."

After this most curious but revealing scene, Bligh says that he challenged anyone who had a complaint against him to step forward, and that Ledward, the surgeon, Hallet, the midshipman, and Cole, the boatswain, did so and were ordered into the Dutchmen's boat. Fryer's account differs here: he says that Bligh ordered Mr. Samuel to write down what he, Fryer, had said against Bligh, that all the officers were to sign the account as correct, and that, if any refused, they were to be sent ashore under arrest. Ledward, Hallet, and Cole got into the boat, followed by Purcell and Fryer, under a torrent of abuse and threats from Bligh, who accompanied his invective with the waving of his bayonet.

The Dutch apparently were not much impressed by the spectacle and did not take Bligh's rages at surface value, for next day the commandant came to Fryer and put pressure on him to make up the quarrel with Bligh; and Fryer duly wrote a letter to Bligh, which began: "I understand from what the Commandant says that matters can be settled. I wish to make everything agreeable as far as lay in my power, that nothing might happen when we came home. . . ." That last phrase was double-edged—it referred to Bligh as well as Fryer.

In his first flush of fury, Bligh noted: "A court was ordered in the morning to enquire into the busyness and at my request they were all separately confined—The master and carpenter as prisoners for tryal when I arrived in Europe, but the others to hear their complaints." In due course, he did bring Purcell before a court martial, but never a word, once he had him in England, did he ever say against Fryer. Because, if he did, something might happen to Bligh as well as to Fryer. What that something was is not difficult to guess. And Bligh was to be sharply reminded of it.

The Dutch commandant came to Bligh and told him officially that Fryer had in his possession a document—which the commandant himself had seen—showing the actual prices which Bligh had paid for provisions and services at Timor. That paper was signed as correct by an official of the town, the Opperlooft of Timor, William Adriaan Van Este. Fryer stated that this paper would prove that Bligh "had made extravagant charges to Government" and that he "would be roughly handled for it" on his return to England. Bligh's heart must have been in his boots for a moment. But he brazened it out, showing the commandant his account books, "signed by the master and boatswain and witnessed by two respectable residanters." That sufficed for the commandant, but it might not have sufficed with an accountant—and one remembers an echo here of how Fryer, previously, on board the *Bounty,* had been forced against his will to sign account books and how he had publicly stated that he was signing because he was ordered to, and that the matter might be reopened later.

The three men who had stood their ground against Bligh—Cole, Hallet, and Ledward—were strangely laconic and noncommital at the court of enquiry held in Sourabaya; or perhaps it was not so strange, as that court consisted of the commandant, the commandant's brother, and another Dutch official. Probably they did not want to wash any more dirty British linen in front of a foreign public; and for their part, the Dutch seemed reluctant to press them too hard. The only embarrassing question was one put to Hallet. "Why did you say to an English sailor now in the service of Holland at this place, that it would not go well with your captain when he returned, he having ill treated every person under his command, for which reason he would be tied to the mouth of a cannon and fired into the air?" Hallet said he didn't remember saying it, but that if he had, he was drunk. Ledward never even mentioned the business about the will, of which he wrote his uncle. Cole said he alleged no particular complaint against Bligh, "God forbid." They were then allowed to return on board the *Resource.*

But there was still the matter of Fryer and Purcell, particularly Fryer. Bligh must have thought hard about that. By reading between the lines of his report, we can see what he did. "I saw the master, when like a villain who had done every mischief he could, and going to receive punishment for it, he trembled, look'd pale, and humbly asked to be forgiven, declaring he would make every concession and disavowal of the infamous reports that he spread. That he would give every reparation I pleased to ask, but I ordered him away on board the prow, telling him that he was to converse no other way with me but by writing and that all his concessions and disavowal of what he had already asserted must be by letter." Once Fryer had done that, he would no longer have had a hold over Bligh; and Bligh could have done with him what he liked. What really happened is obvious from what Bligh *did:* he released Fryer from arrest, but said he would not have him in the ship, he would have to make the next stage of the voyage home in a native craft. Purcell, however, was kept under arrest. The unfortunate carpenter possessed no documents incriminating his captain.

Obviously, Fryer's "concessions" were not obtained by bullying, as Bligh implies, but by bargaining. The master must have agreed to suppress his documents providing Bligh dropped his charges. From Fryer's point of view, although he had lost the chance of revenge, he had achieved something much more important—the salvage of his career. There is no future for an officer who brings charges against his superior—even if the charges are justified—for he will be marked down as a troublesome fellow. Furthermore, Fryer was inarticulate, and painfully conscious of it; he would be at a marked disadvantage, in a court of law, with the glib and quickthinking Bligh. And Bligh had powerful friends at home, whereas Fryer was merely a warrant officer; there would be no repercussions if he was thrown on the scrapheap. And his family would starve.

The *Resource* left Sourabaya on September 17 and arrived at Samarang on the 22nd—the same day as that on which Fletcher Christian brought the *Bounty* to anchor in Matavai Bay. In the first week of October, Bligh reached Batavia, and sold the *Resource*—for once, he lost money on the deal, or so he says—and he also sold the *Bounty's* launch, rather regretfully. From here on, his crew would separate—going home in whatever ship could take them, three here, two there. Some would never go home. Hall, Elphinstone, and Linkletter died at Batavia, having never really recovered from the sufferings of the open boat voyage. Bligh had alleged that Elphinstone was not sick, but "beastly drunk" at Sourbaya; it seems that he wronged the man. Lamb died during his passage home, and Ledward was lost at sea; Nelson had died at Timor; and poor, brave John Norton was dead long ago, on a Pacific island, trying to save the others.

Bligh, of course, was first away from Batavia; sailing in the Dutch ship *Vlydte* accompanied by Mr. Samuel and his servant, John Smith. He had left a trail of scandalous and unsavoury incidents from one end of the Dutch East Indies to the other. It is not surprising that his first act, on arriving at Cape Town, was to write to his backer, Sir Joseph Banks, assuring him that, whatever had happened, anywhere, at any time, it was not Bligh's fault: "In this you will find, sir, the misfortunes of a man who pledges his honour to you, could not be foreseen or guarded against, whose conduct will bear the test of the minutest enquiry, and who only regrets that you should see him so unsuccessful. But altho I have failed in the completion of my undertaking, I had accomplished most assuredly the most difficult part of it. My sufferings have been very great . . ."

He was desperately eager to get home, to present his side of the case *first*. But he had another good reason—the climate of Batavia, which Hamilton was to call "this painted sepulchre, this golgotha of Europe, which buries the whole settlement every five years." To Fryer, he left the responsibility of clearing up the mess; he was to explain Bligh's absence by "certifying that I sailed to the Cape of Good Hope before you, in a packet that could not take any more men, my health being so exceedingly impaired, as to render my existence very doubtful, and that the Governor-General could not give us all a passage in one ship." He said nothing about the health of Mr.

Samuel or his servant, John Smith, who, with him, took the first three available berths home. As commanding officer, Bligh's plain duty was to send home first, away from mosquito-ridden Batavia, the three most seriously ill men; the men who died. But he did not; he left them to die.

As Bligh neared England, the number of the alleged mutineers grew. Soon, he was writing ahead to those of his friends who were influential, that the only members of his whole crew who were worth anything were two in number—Mr. Samuel, his clerk, and Hayward, the midshipman who had "fled into his arms, shedding a torrent of tears".

On March 13, 1790, he watched from the deck of the *Vlydte* the long Bill of Portland rise up out of the sea, like a dragon crouched behind a barrier of racing waters. On the evening of the next day, he transferred from the Dutch ship to an Isle of Wight boat, which swiftly took him in to Portsmouth. There again was the Spithead anchorage, where the *Bounty* had waited so many weary weeks to sail, with Bligh impatient to begin the voyage which, he calculated, would bring him some little fame and certain promotion. It was all exactly as it had been before—even the masts of the sunken *Royal George* were still there, an impediment to navigation and a disgrace to the Admiralty (who had very good reasons for not raising her). And further over, somewhere among the huddled chimneys of Portsea, was the house where his wife had stayed during those wet December weeks—the house to which, with the connivance of Lord Hood, he had slipped away for a final visit to his "dear Betsy," although he was under immediate sailing orders.

Now he was back home in England again. His various despatches and letters had preceded him, all telling the story, not always as he saw it, but as he wished it to be known. It was sensational. The gallant Bligh, alone of all the officers and crew, defying the mutineers to do their worst, even when the villain Christian had a bayonet held at his throat; the pirates sailing off with the ship into the South Seas, leaving their captain marooned in a small boat thousands of miles from the nearest port; alone and unaided, bringing his suffering followers home after a voyage of such distance and duration that there was simply no precedent for it, despite bitter privation and frequent attacks by the natives of the cannibal islands. There was enough truth in Bligh's story to elicit genuine admiration from his contemporaries; and on March 17 Lieutenant Bligh was presented to the King. Even more marvellous, for once the victim of a mutiny had survived to tell his story—usually, they didn't, they got slung overboard—and the public were aching to hear it. The Admiralty publicity department, a very efficient organisation, which worked hard to popularise life in the Navy and sell the brand image of the gay, resourceful, unbeatable British seaman by such methods as subsidising popular song writers, were on the ball at once. Publication of a book by Bligh was authorised by the Lords Commissioners of the Admiralty within a matter of days. Serial rights were sold to the *London Chronicle,* which announced on April 1, the forthcoming publication of Lieutenant Bligh's "Journal of his wonderful escape at sea, in an open boat, for 49 days". In June, Bligh was on the bookstalls—a quick re-hash of his log book, with what nowadays would be regarded as the libellous parts edited out. Consequently, although no one stopped to think about it, the mutiny was inexplicable. There was no hint of trouble in the ship until Bligh had been seized in his cabin that fateful morning; no hint of trouble in the boat; no mention at all of the Sourabaya mutiny. The whole thing was put down to sex. The mutineers had wanted to rejoin their licentious Tahitian lovelies. And Sex Sold. Bligh became, not only a hero, but a best-selling author; and was able to spend the period of his sick leave counting his royalties and plaguing the Admiralty with claims for loss of maps, books, and personal kit, including three dozen shirts at 14*s.* each and one dozen nightcaps at 1*s.* 6*d.* His lost clothing bill came to the staggering total of £121 12*s.* 0*d.* Perhaps he thought he could cash in on his popularity; if so, he was mistaken—the Admiralty disallowed the lot. He then put in a claim for the Tahitian pigs which he had seized from the crew to salt down as rations. The Victualling Board replied, acidly, that this was "a speculation common in the Pursery line and not at the Charge and risk of the Government." And nothing that Bligh wrote could move them.

Meanwhile, the national indignation at the seizure of one of His Majesty's ships by armed mutineers had already been soothed by an announcement in the *London Chronicle* on April 1. "It is said that by the express command of His Majesty two new sloops of war are to be instantly fitted to go in pursuit of the pirates who have taken possession of the *Bounty*. An experienced officer will be appointed to superintend the little command, and the sloops will steer a direct course to Otaheite where, it is conjectured, the mutinous crew have established their rendezvous."

In October, by which time Fryer and the survivors of the boat voyage had arrived in England, the ex-captain of the *Bounty* was tried by court martial for the loss of his ship. The trial took place aboard H.M.S. *Royal William,* then lying at Spithead within a short distance of the spot where the *Bounty* herself had been anchored almost three years before. The president was the Hon. Samuel Barrington, Admiral of the Blue, and second-in-command at Portsmouth. The proceedings were very brief. Although the pertinent questions were asked, the replies were not probed. The court knew that Bligh and his men had been through a staggering ordeal—their faces showed it—and so they were probably more sympathetic than they should perhaps have been.

Each witness was asked: "Did Captain Bligh and the rest of you use your best endeavours to recover her?" They all answered that they had done everything in their power to retake the *Bounty*. The court did not press them by asking what, exactly, they had done.

Bligh was then asked the stock question: "Have you any objection or complaint to make against any of your officer's and Ship's Company now present?" Without a blush, Bligh said that he had none—apart from the charge of insolence and disobedience he had already brought against Purcell.

The court then put to the other officers and men the stock question: "Have you any objection or complaint to make against Lieutenant Bligh?" They all, including Fryer, replied: "None."

The court then honourably acquitted them all; Purcell was quickly wheeled in, charged by Bligh, found guilty in part, and reprimanded.

Through the stern windows of the *Royal William,* a great fleet could be seen assembling at Spithead—for there was a war scare on. Into that fleet slipped a low-built, fast-looking warship—H.M.S. *Pandora,* frigate, 24 guns, 160 men. The men were mostly hastily recruited landsmen, many of them tossing in their hammocks with the gaol fever, transmitted among them from infected clothing, thought her surgeon, Mr. George Hamilton. She was commanded by Captain Edward Edwards, a severe disciplinarian—"*that* Edwards", he was to be called contemptuously by his brother captains. His mission was to seek out the *Bounty* in the South Seas, retake her, and bring Fletcher Christian and the mutineers back alive—for trial. Captain Edwards was grimly determined to effect the capture, to crush mutiny and insubordination with an iron hand; but he had his reservations about the latter part of the instruction. They were guilty, every man jack of them who had stayed aboard the *Bounty* with that villain Christian; a trial was a pure formality. He would take no risk with them—when he caught them.

A few days after Bligh had been honourably acquitted by the court martial, another naval author took up his pen to begin a narrative which was also to sell. "Everything necessary being completed, and an additional complement of naval stores received for the refitment of the *Bounty* . . ." wrote surgeon Hamilton, "we arrived at Portsmouth, and found there Lord Howe with the Union Flag at the main and the proudest navy that ever graced the British seas under his command. Here the officers and men received six months pay in advance, and after receiving their final orders, got the timekeeper on board, weighed anchor, and proceeded to sea."

The voyage of the *Pandora* had begun. In its way, it was to be as epic as that of the *Bounty*. She sailed with a parting prophecy from Bligh, who repeatedly told his relative, the Reverend James Bligh: "Edwards will never return; he does not know the navigation of Endeavour Straits."

Pitcairn Island – the village. From an old print. *Photo: Alexander McKee*

Christian's house on Pitcairn. From an old print. *Photo: Alexander McKee*

Thursday October Christian, son of Fletcher Christian. From an old print. *Photo: Alexander McKee*

John Adams (alias Alexander Smith). From an old print. *Photo: Alexander McKee*

The tomb of William Bligh in a London churchyard. He died in 1817. *Photo: Alexander McKee*

11

"*Pandora's Box*"

WHEN the *Pandora* sailed from Spithead, carrying Hayward with her, presumably for the identification of the mutineers, the party of sixteen which had landed at Matavai Bay from the *Bounty* had been living in their South Sea island paradise for a little over a year. They had split up according to their inclination and were now occupying themselves in different ways. The young midshipman, Peter Heywood (he was sixteen at the time of the mutiny) wrote that, "the morning after the *Bounty* had anchored, my messmate [Mr. Stewart] and I went on shore to the house of an old landed proprietor, our former friend; and being now set free from a lawless crew, determined to remain as much apart from them as possible, and wait patiently for the arrival of a ship." Stewart, a slender youth of twenty-three, was one of the two who, Fryer said, had "there particular Girls." The majority, it may be inferred, had taken the opportunity of tasting flower after dusky flower. But Stewart's "particular Girl" was probably particular; she was the daughter of a chief, the *tyo* of Stewart and Heywood. This was certainly a love match, Stewart married her soon after his arrival, and gave her the name of Peggy; in due course, she bore him a baby girl. Heywood, however, formed no permanent attachment; he gave most of his attention to the production of an

English/Otaheitan dictionary, which later proved of real value.

Morrison, the other man who had a "particular Girl", cannot have been much attached emotionally. He was older than the two midshipmen, and a well-educated, competent man; he saw no reason to wait possibly years for a ship. He decided to build his own. There was plenty of wood, some iron, and a number of tools; among the sixteen men were the armourer, Coleman, two carpenters, Norman and McIntosh, and the cooper, Hillbrant. Millward and Muspratt, both of them half-hearted mutineers, who had taken up arms for a time when ordered to do so by Churchill, also joined Morrison; in the end, he had ten helpers working hard—to the amazement of the pleasure-loving Tahitians—to build, to his own design, a schooner more than thirty feet long. But only to his closest associates did he confide his design of sailing in her to Batavia; to the others he gave out that the boat was "only for the purposes of Pleasuring about the Island."

The natives crowded round to admire the craft, as month by month it took shape; yes, it would be better than their own canoes, they thought, but wondered "how the seamen could keep at it without being tired."

A little settlement grew up around the improvised boatyard, a flagstaff was errected "to hoist the collours on Sundays". Morrison read Divine service on that day, and the natives "always behaved with much decency when present at our worship, tho they could not understand one word."

The impending problems of navigation were partly solved when Morrison got hold of a quadrant, belonging to Hallet, which one of the hard-core mutineers, Matthew Thompson, had taken; but Thompson would not give up to him some nautical books which had belonged to Hayward. Thompson, who was a surly man of forty, lived apart from the rest, sharing a billet with Charles Churchill; neither took any interest in the work on the schooner.

Churchill, a dominating personality, was living in state with his *tyo,* a chief called Vayheeadooa. Thompson lived with them as a kind of underprivileged guest. Like attracts like; a frequent visitor to their house was a remarkable character who called himself Brown, but whose name was really Bound. He said he had put ashore from the brig *Mercury,* of London, commanded by Captain J. H. Cox, when she had called at Tahiti shortly before the *Bounty* arrived for the last time; the trouble was, he explained, that he had slashed another member of the crew across the face with a knife. That may have been so, but the ship was formerly the East India Company ship *Gustavus III* on her way to the Sandwich Isles and China. Her captain really was J. H. Cox, who described Brown (or Bound) as "an Ingenious handy Man when sober, but when Drunk a dangerous fellow."

How had he come to be in the Swedish Navy? According to Brown, his career had been not without incident. He had been a sergeant of Marines at Portsmouth. Then, being "broke" from the service for a crime he did not specify, he had shipped in a frigate to India, joined the forces of Hyder Ali as an officer and turned Mohammedan. Having tired of this, he deserted, joined with some other adventurers in the seizure and plunder of an East India Company vessel, been tried for it and escaped conviction. On being sent back to England, he had found the country too hot to hold him, and had eventually joined the *Mercury*. Or so he said.

About the toughness of Thompson, however, there was no doubt at all; only the brawny, brazen harlots of Portsmouth Town could cope with his type. The amatory technique practised in the brothels of "Spice Island" gave grave offence on Tahiti when employed on the daughter of a chief. The girl's brother came to her assistance, knocked Thompson sprawling, and then ran off. In a vile temper, Thompson returned to his hut. He found a crowd of curious natives, mostly strangers, eager for their first sight of an Englishman. Thompson bawled at them to go away—in English. As they stared at him uncomprehendingly, he levelled his musket and pulled the trigger. A man and his child were killed, a woman had her jaw broken.

In March, by which time Morrison and his party had completed the frame of their schooner, Churchill was elevated to the position of a native chief. His *tyo,* Vayheeadooa, had died. There were no children; and by Tahitian custom, the name of the chief, his position, and his property, became Churchill's. The big, burly, ex-ship's corporal took to the position as to the manner born; he was a man-manager by training and inclination, and popular with the natives. The loutish Thompson, ten years older than Churchill, thought that his mate was getting a bit above himself; there were quarrels.

About a month later Churchill broke his collar bone while out duck shooting. Burkett, another of the hard-core mutineers, helped him back to his house; Thompson was there, and Burkett stayed the night with them. Next morning, while Burkett was outside the house, he heard the sound of a single musket shot.

He ran back to it, and saw Thompson standing in the doorway, loading a musket. Thompson glared at him and asked him if he was angry. Burkett, being unarmed, could only say "No." Then, looking at the musket, he added, "I hope you don't mean to take advantage of me." "No," growled Thompson, "not without you are angry." He nodded his head towards the interior of the house. "I've done him."

Looking through the doorway, Burkett saw the ex-ship's corporal of the *Bounty* lying on the floor. There was a small hole torn in his back, where the musket ball had entered, and an enormous, gaping bloody wound in his chest, where it had come out, having gone right through him.

Burkett hastily buried Churchill and then set off home, to compose a letter to Morrison. The contents have survived (through quotation in Morrison's expanded narrative), preserving the dialogue exactly; including the catch-phrase about Thompson having "done" Churchill.

The news of the murder spread quickly; Thompson was surprised and flattered to see a small group of natives, led by a Tahitian friend of Churchill's called Partirre, approaching him with smiles and calling out to him "Vayheeadooa," meaning that he was now chief of them all in Churchill's place. They crowded round him, five or six of them, congratulating him. Then, when Partirre, who was a large, strong man, had manoeuvred himself between Thompson and Thompson's musket, he suddenly lashed out with his fist and knocked Thompson down. As Thompson lay sprawling, another native picked up a plank which happened to be inside the house, thrust it across Thompson's body, and two of them sat on it to hold him down.

Thompson's struggles lasted only for the space of time it took Partirre to dash outside, pick up a large stone, and return with it. Then he calmly and methodically hammered Thompson's head in. They buried the murderer's body, but cut off the head first. When the skull was shown later to Surgeon Hamilton, he wrote that it "bore evident marks of fracture".

On hearing the news, Morrison went to Tinah to find out the details; Partirre told him what had happened, saying, "Don't be angry that it was I who killed him, seeing that he had killed my chief and my friend." Morrison was not at all angry. "I looked on him as the instrument in the Hand of Providence to punish such Crimes," he wrote.

By July 1, Morrison's schooner was ready for launching. A party of 400 men hauled it three-quarters of a mile to the beach. It was floated and named *Resolution*. The difficulty now was to obtain sails. By taking part in a native war, they won as a reward enough matting to make some sails, of a sort. They then set out on a number of trial trips round the islands, their home-made schooner, little larger than Bligh's boat, performing like a thoroughbred; later on, she became well-known in the Pacific and the China Sea as a very swift sailer. But with only the flimsy matting for sails, her chances of weathering a gale in dangerous, reef-strewn waters were minute. Morrison and his companions postponed their sailing date for Batavia, and laid her up for the winter under an improvised shelter.

The campaigning season in Tahiti began in March, when the rains ceased; on March 1, 1791, the *Resolution* was put into the water, and on March 21, she sailed to take part in a native war, on the side of their Tahitian friends. In her went Morrison, Norman, Ellison, Byrn, McIntosh, Millward, and Hillbrant; on their way, they picked up Burkett, Sumner, Muspratt, and the man who called himself Brown. Four Europeans only remained in the Matavai Bay area—the midshipmen Heywood and Stewart in their self-imposed segregation; Coleman, one of the men who had wanted to go with Bligh; and Skinner, who had tried to shoot Bligh.

On the morning of March 23, as Heywood was setting off for an expedition in the mountains with two Tahitian friends, he saw the long-expected, but by now unbelievable, sight of a European ship working into the bay. Three tall masts and a single row of grinning gunports, twelve a-side: a frigate. H.M.S. *Pandora.* He ran madly down the hill to join Stewart on the beach, and they immediately scrambled into a canoe. Coleman had been nearer to the point for which the frigate was making; he launched his canoe, but a strong breeze overturned it, and he swam the remaining distance. Skinner was away, out of sight of the bay, and did not know.

Surgeon Hamilton was seeing Tahiti for the first time—the blue water, the greenery, the high, conical mountains of the interior standing up like pyramids under a brassy sky, in a hot, glittering light. Then he saw his first native canoe, flashing across the water towards the slowly moving European ship. "The native came on board, and showed expressions of joy to a degree of madness, on embracing and saluting us, by whom we learnt that several of the mutineers were on the island; but that Mr. Christian and nine men had left Otaheite long since, in the *Bounty*. Language cannot express his surprise on Lieutenant Hayward's being introduced to him, who had been purposely concealed."

Joseph Coleman, swimming like a madman, flashed alongside the frigate as she bore slowly on through the water; and was taken aboard even before the mooring buoy had been streamed. Dazed with happiness, he was taken before Captain Edwards, knowing that Bligh had promised to do him justice. Edwards soon had the story out of him: some of the *Bounty's* crew were living near Matavai Bay, others had gone off in a schooner they had built, Churchill and Thompson were dead, the *Bounty* had been twice at Tahiti since the mutiny. That was the question that interested Edwards. Where was the *Bounty?* Coleman could only say that she was last seen steering N.W.

Shortly after, Heywood and Stewart were seen coming out in their double canoe. As they stood at last on the neat, scrubbed quarter-deck of the warship, with its meticulously ordered gear and fancy paint, they felt uneasily self-conscious. To the officers and seamen waiting to receive them, they must have appeared to have gone native, for they were burned brown by the sun and tattooed in the Tahitian manner, as this, among their hosts, had been a mark of dignity and honour. It was two years since the mutiny. That all seemed a very long time ago. Heywood said, in an embarrassed fashion, to the senior officer present, Lieutenant Larkin, "I suppose you know my story?" As Larkin did not reply, Heywood added, "I belong to the *Bounty*."

He and Stewart were taken down at once to Captain Edwards' cabin. Edwards asked, grimly: "What news?"

"I suppose you have heard of the affair of the *Bounty*, sir?"

Edwards replied that that was the very purpose of his coming to Tahiti; to arrest the mutineers, keep them as closely confined as possible, and bring them home to undergo due punishment. The bottom appeared to fall out of Heywood's world—Edwards seemed to think him guilty. It was his grim, uncompromising attitude, more than anything he said, which conveyed the fact that he had, already, mentally condemned Heywood to death as a mutineer. Immensely agitated, he gave Edwards a bad impression by constantly interrupting him, to assert his innocence; then both he and Stewart asked to see Hayward. They knew he was on board, the native had told them; Hayward knew the facts, he could bear out the truth of what they said. Edwards then signalled for Hayward to come out of the neighbouring stateroom, where he had been sent by Edwards, to eavesdrop. And Hayward, resplendent now in lieutenant's uniform—a change, it has been said, "from a filthy maggot to a shining butterfly"—confronted his former midshipmen friends.

Edwards recorded that he treated them to "a sort of contemptuous look"; Heywood wrote that "he (like all worldlings when raised a little in life) received us very coolly, and pretended ignorance of our affairs."

Edwards immediately called out for Lieutenant Larkin, and ordered him to put the two surrendered midshipmen in irons. Someone, probably Edwards, called them "piratical villains"; and Heywood heatedly replied that he hoped to vindicate his conduct.

Coleman was already in irons; Skinner, as soon as he came aboard, was also put in irons; and two boats were put into the water, under Lieutenant Corner and Lieutenant Hayward, to pursue Morrison's schooner. Edwards had assumed that, because she had gone (actually to take part in a native war), that it was an attempted escape on the part of more of these piratical villains. Byrn, while ashore from the schooner at Paparra, about twenty-four miles away, heard the news of the *Pandora's* arrival from the natives, and walked all through the night to get to her, and give himself up. The half-blind Irishman was put in irons, too.

Meanwhile, the two boats under Corner and Hayward had abandoned the pursuit of Morrison's schooner as hopeless. They had sighted her on the previous evening, had closed to within a mile; and then the home-made vessel had clapped on sail and left them standing. Morrison produced a story to explain this, saying that he intended to sail up to the *Pandora* openly and surrender himself; he did not intend to put himself in the invidious position of being captured by the ship's boats, which would have told heavily against him. But probably there was more to it than this; because as soon as the boats had given up, he closed the shore and landed Burkett, Sumner, Muspratt, Milward, Hillbrant, and McIntosh. This party immediately made off into the hills. All except McIntosh were implicated in some way in the mutiny. Once free of them, Morrison left his schooner at anchor by the shore—possibly for the use of the other men if they wanted it—and, accompanied only by Norman and the youngster Ellison, walked along the beach towards the *Pandora*. After covering about a dozen miles, they came on Corner's boat, with the lieutenant and his men fast asleep. Morrison rather unfeelingly woke them up, in order to surrender to them. However, when taken back to the *Pandora,* this party also was put in irons. Edwards was carrying out to the letter his instructions not to let any of the mutineers escape; and in his eyes, anyone who had been in contact with mutineers was likely to have become contaminated. He had himself already had experience of a mutiny, aboard H.M.S. *Narcissus* in 1782, and was determined to stamp out the virus.

The capture of the ex-*Bounty* men who were marching into the interior, to seek protection from a native chief, proved more difficult. Hayward, in charge of one landing party, pursued them from the shore; while Corner, who had been an Army officer, led a second party seeking to get between the mutineers and the mountains. The seamen, a motley lot—the dregs brought in by the Press Gang after a major swoop to get men for the important war fleet preparing for sea under Lord Howe—baulked repeatedly at the frequent river crossings or were swept away by the current; but their native guides went over with ease, swimming the fast water like otters. Finally, Corner managed to cut off the retreat of the *Bounty's* men, while Hayward came at them from the other direction.

Hayward made contact during the night, using the services of Brown (or Bound), who had now embarked on a further adventure in his eventful career, signing on as an A.B. in the *Pandora*. Brown had gone native, could make himself understood in Tahitian, and, wrote Hamilton, "from natural complexion was much darker than any of the natives." Going forward during the night to scout for his former friends, he came "creeping up to the place where they were asleep, distinguishing them from the natives by feeling their toes; as people unaccustomed to wear shoes are easily discovered from the spread of their toes."

In the morning, Hayward's party advanced on the hut, calling on the men to lay down their arms; they did so, offering no resistance—and the last of the *Bounty's* men remaining in Tahiti were prisoners. There had been two casualties. A native had thrown a stone at the woman of one of the mutineers, and the seaman had promptly shot him dead. The other incident worried Edwards. There had been a native attack on one of the landing parties, in which another Tahitian had been killed. There was constant danger that his prisoners might be rescued by the natives, for they were the friends of the most influential chiefs; the Tahitians were very angry. He had to keep close watch on the *Pandora's* moorings, in case of an attempt by native assault swimmers to cut them and so wreck the frigate. And, equally important, his own scratch crew had to be deterred from desertion and mutiny.

He also had on his mind the problem of accommodating his prisoners in such a way that they could neither infect his crew with the disease of mutiny nor have any chance of escape. The solution he hit on was, he wrote, a "round house which I built at the after part of the quarter-deck for their more effectual security, airy and healthy situation." Hamilton, his surgeon, adds that it was "the most desirable place in the ship," and that the prisoners were put on full rations instead of the reduced allowance normally given. This construction, inevitably, was nicknamed "Pandora's Box". The catch was, the space inside measured only 18 feet by 11 feet, and into it were put fourteen men, with irons on their legs and handcuffs, newly made by the armourer, on their wrists. They were, as Heywood wrote, "obliged to eat, drink, sleep, and obey the calls of nature here."

Morrison was more explicit. "The centrys were placed on the top, while the midshipman walk'd across by the bulk head, and here no person was suffered to speak to us but the master-at-arms, and his orders was not to speak to us on any score but that of our provisions. The heat of the place when it was calm was so intense that the sweat frequently ran in streams to the scuppers, and produced maggots in a short time, the hammocks being dirty when we got them, we found stored with vermin of another kind, which we had no method of erradicating but by lying on the plank; and our only remedy was to lay naked."

Worse was to come, for as the wretched men turned and stirred restlessly in their handcuffs and leg-irons one sultry Pacific night, McIntosh managed to get one leg out of his shackle. The officer of the watch discovered it, and a general examination took place, "when the leg irons were reduced to fit close, and Mr. Larkin, the first Lieut., in trying the handcuffs, took the method of setting his foot against our breasts and hauling the handcuffs over our hands with all his might, some of which took the skin off with them, and all that could be haul'd off by this means were reduced, and fitted so close, that there was no possibility of turning the hand in them, and when our wrists began to swell, he told us that 'they were not intended to fit like gloves.' "

The wives and girl friends of the unfortunate prisoners were wild with grief. According to an account written six years afterwards during the missionary voyage of the *Duff*, Peggy Stewart, taking her newly-born baby with her, had been allowed to see her husband when he was first imprisoned. But "the interview was so affecting and afflicting, that the officers on board were overwhelmed with anguish, and Stewart himself, unable to bear the heart-rending scene, begged she might not be admitted again on board. She was separated from him by violence, and conveyed on shore in a state of despair . . . Withheld from him, and forbidden to come any more on board, she sunk into the deepest dejection, dying literally of a broken heart. Her child is yet alive . . ."

This final meeting between Stewart and his wife and child most probably occurred soon after his arrest, and without the authority of the strict Edwards and his bully, Larkin, the First Lieutenant. We know that Lieutenant Corner was sympathetic to the prisoners; possibly he may have engineered it. Surgeon Hamilton does not mention this incident, but he does make clear that only their children were permitted to visit: "The prisoners wives visited the ship daily, and brought their children, who were permitted to be carried to their unhappy fathers. To see the poor captives in irons, weeping over their tender offspring, was too moving a scene for any feeling heart. Their wives brought them ample supplies of every delicacy that the country afforded, and behaved with the greatest fidelity and affection to them."

The reason for forbidding the wives to see their husbands was probably to prevent a rescue attempt being made by the *tyos* of the imprisoned men. One such attempt was in active preparation, according to Hamilton: "Oripai, the king's brother, discovered a conspiracy amongst the natives on shore to cut our cables should it come to blow hard from the sea." The thought of the *Pandora,* pounding in the surf, the powder wet, facing a yelling rush by a horde of native spearmen and sling-throwers must have been at the back of Edwards' mind. So far, he had done well; but not well enough. The ring-leader, Christian, and the *Bounty* herself, had escaped him. However, he stayed on at Tahiti until May 8, prolonging the agony, as Morrison shows: "During the time we staid, the weomen with whom we had cohabited on the island came frequently under the stern (bringing their children, of which there were 6 born, four girls and two boys, and several of the weomen big with child) cutting their heads till the blood discoloured the water about them . . . but when they came to be known, they were always driven away by the Captn's orders and none of them sufferd to come near the ship."

Some of the prisoners, by this time, were in a bad way. "Coleman's legs, being much swell'd, he was let out of irons, as was also Norman and Byrn on their falling sick, but they were always handcuff'd at night. McIntosh and Ellison's arms being much gall'd by their irons had them taken off till they should get well, but their legs were still kept fast," wrote Morrison. Coleman and McIntosh were among the three (Norman was the other) whom Bligh had specifically stated "were kept against their consent & are deserving Mercy." Against the half-blind fiddler's name in his "Description List," Bligh had written: "Michael Byrn I was told has no knowledge of what he was doing." It made no difference to Edwards, they were all guilty until declared innocent by a court martial. They were all mutineers; and, besides, their fate would provide a salutary example to his own crew of newly-lifted landsmen.

Morrison's schooner, the *Resolution,* was put into commission as a tender to help scout for the *Bounty*. The command of her was, wrote Hamilton, "given to Mr. Oliver the master's mate, Mr. Renouard a midshipman, James Dodds a quartermaster; and six privates were put on board of her." "She was decked, beautifully built, and the size of a Gravesend boat."

As the *Pandora* slowly put out from Tahiti, "with a pleasant breeze," accompanied by the little *Resolution,* none guessed at the epic adventure ahead.

12

"*Edwards Will Never Return*"

Edward Edwards, R.N., Post-Captain of nine years seniority, was, in his own eyes, a severely just man; he was also an unimaginative one. He made a number of deductions concerning the whereabouts of the *Bounty,* and he managed to be hopelessly wrong each time. He wandered aimlessly about the Pacific for four months, following vague clues; and the only evidence he found of her existence was early in the search, on May 22, when Lieutenant Corner found on the beach at Palmerston's Isle some spars marked with the Government broad arrow and the name *Bounty.* Edwards though he was hot on her trail; and sent off the boats to inspect other islands close by. Lieutenants Corner and Hayward made a kind of swimming reconnaissance of each island. Burdened with arms and ammunition, but buoyed up by cork life-jackets, they swam through the heavy surf to the beaches. But they drew blank, for the spars were not evidence that the *Bounty* had been there. They had in fact drifted down many hundreds of miles with the prevailing current from the place where they had been lost nearly two years before—during Christian's abortive attempt to settle on Tubai.

Believing that he was about to lay hands on Christian and the *Bounty,* Edwards ruthlessly drove his men, although the weather was freshening and becoming dangerous for boat work. Midshipman Sival came alongside in the tiny jolly boat, was told that he had not fully carried out his orders, and that he must go back at once and rectify his mistakes; as he cast off, someone thoughtfully threw a piece of salt beef down into the boat, knowing that the men had had no food all day. Bobbing like a cork on the rising sea, the little craft vanished into the driving murk which had already blotted out all sign of the shore; and was never seen or heard of again. Alone in the Pacific, with one piece of beef, and no water—sent to their deaths for the sake of a false deduction.

Hamilton noted in his journal that "by these accidents the Divine Ruler of the universe has peopled the southern hemisphere," and went on to make a penetratingly accurate observation of Christian's probable intentions: "Although that unfortunate man has, in a rash unguarded moment, been tempted to swerve from his duty to his king and country, as he is in other respects of an amiable character, and respectable abilities, should he elude the hand of justice, it may be hoped he will enjoy his talents in humanizing the rude savages; so that, at some future period, a British Lion may blaze forth with all the characteristic virtues of the English nation, and complete the great prophecy, by propagating the Christian knowledge among the infidels. As Christian has taken fourteen beautiful women with him from Otaheite, there is little doubt of his intention of colonising some undiscovered island." That is just what Christian had done—added another possession to the growing British Empire, although in a stranger manner than the surgeon could guess.

Exactly a month after losing the jolly boat, Edwards lost the *Resolution* also. On this day, June 22, according to Hamilton, "One woman amongst many others came on board. She was six feet high, of exquisite beauty, and exact symmetry, being naked, and unconscious of her being so, added a lustre to her charms. Many mouths were watering for her; but Captain Edwards, with great humanity and prudence, had given previous orders, that no women should be permitted to go below, as our health had not quite recovered the shock it received at Otaheite. It now came on to blow fresh, and we were obliged to make off from the land. At five o'clock in the evening we lost sight of our tender. False fires were burnt, and great guns and small arms were fired without success, as it came on thick blowing weather. What was most unfortunate, water and provisions were then on deck for her, which were intended to have been put on board of her in the morning." And the schooner, too, had been abandoned without food or water; nine more British seamen lost in the wastes of the Pacific, with thousand of miles between them and the nearest European haven.

As the frigate, battered by the gale, deluged with rain gusts, pitched and rolled onwards to the Friendly Isles, the wretched prisoners, some of them sweating with a temperature, slithered wildly about the deck of their cage to the limit of their chains. "Our miserable situation," wrote Morrison, "soon brought sickness on amongst us and the Surgeon (Mr. Hamilton), a very humane gentleman, gave us all the assistance in his power, but at the same time informed us that Captn Edwards had given such orders that it was out of his power to be of any service to us in our present circumstances. However, between him and the second Lieut., a copper kettle was provided to boil our cocoa in, which was served with sugar in lieu of butter and cheese—and this with the Divine providence kept us alive. As the place was washed twice a week, we were wash'd with it, there being no room to shift us from place to place . . . and when the roughness of the weather gave the ship any motion, we were not able to keep ourselves fast, to remedy which we were threatened to be stapel'd down by the Captain. But Mr. Corner gave us some short boards to check ourselves with, which he made the carpenters secure, and thereby prevented us from maiming each other and ourselves."

On June 29, the *Pandora* anchored at Anamooka in the Friendly Isles. It was on one of these Isles that Bligh's boat had suffered attack and Norton had been killed—the place ever afterwards being dubbed Murderer's Cove. "Murderer's Cove, in the Friendly Isles, is saying a volume on the subject," remarked Hamilton. "The people of Anamooka are the most daring set of robbers in the South Seas. While Captain Edwards was ashore, distributing presents, he sent a seaman back to the boat alone. As soon as he got out of our sight, they stripped him naked, and robbed him of his cloaths, and every article he had, but one shoe, which he used for concealing his nakedness. Lieut. Hayward called the assistance of the guard in searching for the robbers. We saw the natives all running, and dodging behind the trees, which led us to suspect that there was some mischief brewing; but we soon discovered the great Irishman, with his shoe full in one hand, and a bayonet in the other, naked and foaming mad with revenge on the natives, for the treatment he had received."

Hamilton shows that, despite everything the ruthless Edwards could do, there were many native thieves whom no precaution could stop—a necessary corrective to Bligh's torrent of abuse, whenever a theft occurred, directed at the unfortunate officer or seaman who had been the victim of an islander's cunning. Hamilton also records, with Northumberland gusto, that "many beautiful girls were brought on board for sale, by their mothers, who were very exorbitant in their demands, as nothing less than a broad axe would satisfy them; but after standing their market three days, *la pucelage* fell to an old razor, a pair of scissors, or a very large nail. Had the razors held out, I believe all the girls in the island would have undergone the same operation."

They were now in the actual waters where the mutiny had occurred. "In the night," wrote Hamilton, "the burning mountain of Tofoa exhibited a very grand spectacle." It was the same volcano whose fiery display had kept men up late on the deck of the *Bounty,* and so spoiled Christian's original plan merely to desert.

Edwards now began to wander aimlessly among the islands. He had been grimly confident at Tahiti, where he had swept all the mutineers into his net so easily; he had been ablaze with optimism at the finding of the *Bounty's* spars soon after. Now, he realized how vast the Pacific was, and how many tens of thousands of islands it contained. Only luck—or an accurate divination of Christian's intentions—could help him. In early August, he had his hand on a clue, and did not see it. "We now bore away," wrote Hamilton, "intending to steer in the track of Carteret and Bligh . . ." Carteret, whose book describing his voyage of 1767 Christian had used in order to select a suitable island! Had he continued that course, it would have led him straight to Christian and the *Bounty.*

However, he pursued no methodical plan. Mentally adrift, with the baffled rage of a ruthlessly determined commander to whom, inexplicably, success is not granted, he hardly bothered now to look where he was going. Turning west, directly away from the refuge of the last remaining mutineers, on August 13 he saw, incuriously, a mountainous, wooded island to the north-west "We saw smoke very plain," he reported, "from which it may be presumed that the island is inhabited." He did not bother now even to investigate such signs, of which, a few months earlier, he would have been deeply suspicious. Yet, desperate eyes were watching him—the columns of smoke were almost certainly desperate signals—for, wrecked on the shore, lay the hulk of the French ship *Boussole* and, in deeper water, sunk from sight, the hull of another, *l'Astrolabe.* On the island, known then as Pitt's Island, were the remnants of the expedition led by Jean-François de La Pérouse. They had been there three years, since 1788. The melancholy traces left by the castaways were not found until long after the men had perished. In his present mood, Edwards could have sailed within a mile of Christian's colony, and failed to see it.

And retribution came to him, as swiftly and as unexpectedly, as it had come to Bligh.

It was now August 28. There were unknown reefs, white with surf, stretching in a long line before them. Edwards ordered Lieutenant Corner to take a boat and prospect a passage through them. Corner went to the topmasthead, for a good look around, and then set off. At 5 P.M., just before the swift tropical night fell, the men of the *Pandora* saw Corner's signal that he had found a way through; and then, within a few minutes, daylight gave way to darkness. Impatiently, Edwards signalled for Corner to expedite his return; he directed "false fires" to be burnt and muskets to be fired into the air. Surgeon Hamilton distinctly saw the answering flashes, out in the darkness, of muskets being fired by Corner's men. But Edwards could not wait; he ordered soundings to be taken—got no bottom with a 110-fathom line—and ordered the *Pandora* on into the darkness towards the boat, and the reef. As the boat came bobbing out of the night, steering in towards the stern of the frigate, Edwards ordered soundings again. Instead of "No bottom with this line!" he got "Fifty fathoms!" A coral reef rises steeply up from the abyss of the great depths, but still Edwards drove on. "It had lately been our custom to lay to in the night," explained Hamilton, "M. Bougainville (another of the great French navigators) having represented this part of the ocean as exceedingly dangerous." And now, adds Hamilton, "after we had passed to the westward of Bougainville's track, the ocean was perfectly unexplored." What Edwards was in fact doing was to charge the then unknown Great Barrier Reef head on in total darkness. There was a hoarse, grinding roar and the frigate, turning slowly under full topsails, drifted in among the breakers, reeling crazily so that, wrote Morrison, "with every surge we expected that the masts would go by the board."

Frantically, the chained men, secured inside their bolted and barred prison by leg-irons and handcuffs, tried to wrench themselves free.

Edwards started to roar out orders, in the hope that hull damage was not serious. First, he tried to get the frigate free by sailing her off, setting all canvas—but she continued to bump and grind on the coral heads. Then he had the sails furled and had the boats hoisted out, so that they could carry an anchor well astern of the ship. He hoped that by having the crew haul on the anchor cable, the ship might be pulled to safety. But a shout from the carpenter stopped him—in five minutes, the hold had filled with water to a depth of a foot-and-a-half. Fifteen minutes later, there was nine feet of water in the hold. Only the reef was holding her up.

"At this dreadful crisis," wrote Hamilton, "it blew very violently; and the ship beat so hard upon the rocks, that we expected her, every minute, to go to pieces. It was an exceedingly dark, stormy night; and the gloomy horrors of death presented us all round, being everywhere encompassed with rocks, shoals, and broken water."

"We were in danger at every stroke of killing each other with our irons," wrote Morrison, of the swaying pandemonium inside "Pandora's Box". With the fury of despair they tugged at their shackles. "We broke them that we might be ready to assist ourselves and keep from killing each other, and informed the officers what we had done. When Mr. Corner was acquainted with it, he came aft and we told him we should attempt nothing further, as we only wanted a chance for our lives; which he promised we should have, telling us not to fear."

At about 10 P.M. the ship was driven by the raging surf clear over the reef into the shallow water beyond, rolling and swaying sluggishly with the great weight of water in her, and with more pouring in every second. The crew's exertions now became positively desperate.

"The guns were ordered to be thrown overboard," wrote

Hamilton, "and what hands could be spared from the pumps, were employed thrumbing a topsail to haul under her bottom, to eandeavour to fodder her. At this juncture one of the chain-pumps gave way; and the water gained fast upon us. The scheme of the topsail was now laid aside, and every soul fell to bailing and pumping. We baled between life and death; for had she gone down before daylight, every soul must have perished. She now took a heel, and some of the guns they were endeavouring to throw overboard run down to leeward, which crushed one man to death; about the same time, a spare topmast came down from the booms, and killed another man."

In their narrow prison, lying in total darkness, with the roar of the guns rolling down the decks beneath them, and the thunder of falling masts and spars above, the prisoners waited for death. Edwards must have known that some at least were not really mutineers at all, for how else to explain the choice he now made?

"Coleman, Norman, and McIntosh were ordered out to the pumps, and the boats got out; but as soon as Captain Edwards was informed that we had broke our irons he ordered us to be handcuff'd and leg iron'd again with all the irons that could be mustered, tho' we begged for mercy and desired leave to go to the pumps, but to no purpose, his orders were put into execution," wrote Morrison. "The master-at-arms and corporal were now armed with each a brace of pistols and placed as additional centinals over us, with orders to fire amongst us if we made any motion; and the master-at-arms told us that the Captn had said he would either shoot or hang to the yard arms those who should make any further attempt to break the irons. Having recommended ourselves to the Almighty protection, we lay down and seem'd for a while to forget our miserable situation, tho' we could hear the officers busy getting their things into the boats which were haul'd under the stern on purpose, and heard some of the men on deck say, 'I'll be damn'd if they shall go without us.' This made some of us start, and moving the irons, the master-at-arms said, 'fire upon the rascals.' As he was then just over the scuttle I spoke to him and said 'for God's sake don't fire, what's the matter, there is none here moving.' "

Yet it was vitally necessary to the safety of every soul aboard the *Pandora* to get fresh men to the pumps; for those there already were exhausted. "The people now became faint at the pumps, and it was necessary to give them refreshment," wrote Hamilton. "The men behaved with the utmost intrepidity and obedience, not a man flinching from his post. We continually cheered them at the pumps with the delusive hopes of its being soon daylight." Poor men, many of them pressed; many of them landsmen too young or too old for the battle fleet; many of them sick, unfit to begin with, and diseased from the cramped, insanitary conditions of the long voyage. But none flinched, or gave up hope, or gave way to the terror which must have possessed them, tossed in those tumultuous waves, in a sinking ship, in the middle of a lonely ocean. By daybreak, "the water was coming in faster at the gun-ports than the pumps could discharge; and to this minute the men never swerved from their duty. She now took a very heavy heel, so much so that she quite lay down on one side."

Edwards had spent the last half-hour holding a council of war, securing from his officers a verdict that nothing more could be done to save the ship, and prudently, with a view to the inevitable court martial, having this put down in writing by his clerk and signed by the surgeon and the purser. Then he prepared to abandon ship. The prisoners remaining in "Pandora's Box," by the unanimous testimony of Morrison, and Heywood were still firmly secured by their shackles: and the narrow hatchway down into the "Box" bolted down above their heads.

"The boats," testified Heywood, "by this time had all been prepared; and as the captain and officers were coming upon the poop or roof of our prison, to abandon the ship, the water being then up to the combings of the hatchways, we again implored his mercy."

"We begg'd that we might not be forgot," wrote Morrison. "When by Captn Edwards's order Joseph Hodges, the amourer's mate of the *Pandora,* was sent down to take the irons off Muspratt and Skinner, and send them and Byrn (who was then out of irons) up. But Skinner being too eager to get out, got haul'd up with his handcuffs on, and the other two following him close, the scuttle was shut and bar'd before Hodges could get to it, and he in the meantime knock'd off my hand irons and Stewart's. I beg'd the master-at-arms to leave the scuttle open, when he answer'd 'Never fear, my boys, we'll all go to Hell together.' The words were scarcely out of his mouth when the ship took a sally and a general cry of 'there she goes' was heard, the master-at-arms and corporal with the other centinels roll'd overboard, and at the same instant, we saw through the stern ports Captn Edwards swimming to the pinnace which was yet some distance astern. Burkett and Hillbrant were yet handcuff'd and the ship under water as far as the main mast and it was now beginning to flow in upon us when the Devine providence directed William Moulter (boatswain's mate) to the place. He was scrambling up on the box and hearing our crys took out the bolt and threw it and the scuttle overboard, such was his presence of mind, tho he was forced to follow instantly himself."

Moulter simply lost his footing because the heel of the ship was now so great; she was almost on her beam ends. Captain Edwards had actually been standing on top of the barred prison when he had personally abandoned ship. "One of the officers," reported Hamilton, had then "told the Captain that the anchor on our bow was under water; that she was then going; and bidding him farewell, jumped over the quarter into the water. The Captain then followed his example, and jumped after him. At that instant she took her last heel; and, while everyone were scrambling to windward, she sunk in an instant. The crew had just time to leap overboard, accompanying it with a most dreadful yell. The cries of men drowning in the water was at first awful in the extreme; but as they sunk, and became faint, it died away by degrees."

The prisoners were last out—and not all of them escaped—and of those who did, some were still in handcuffs. Heywood says he was "the last out but three. The water was then pouring in at the bulk-head scuttles, yet I succeeded in getting out, and was scarcely in the sea when I could see nothing above me but the cross trees, and nothing around me but a scene of the greatest distress." He later drew two vivid sketches of those last moments of the *Pandora,* which he sent to his adoring sister, "Nessy" Heywood.

Morrison's impressions were recorded in his journal. "We all got out except Hillbrant though it was full as much as I could do to clear myself of the driver boom before she sunk." Hillbrant, still shackled, went to the bottom of the Pacific inside "Pandora's Box." The unfortunate Skinner, who had rushed up the moment the scuttle was first opened, with his handcuffs on, was sinking slowly down towards the coral, twisting and contorted, with bubbles of air bursting from his mouth. Somewhere beside him, also handcuffed, sank the bodies of Sumner and Stewart, to lie sightless on the coral fifteen fathoms down. With them, lay thirty-five of the *Pandora's* own crew. Thirty-five. Although Edwards had had eleven hours, from the moment of the frigate's striking, to prepare to abandon ship. Thirty-nine lives in all, lost because of a burst of impatience which made Captain Edward Edwards, R.N., set his ship at an unexplored, uncharted coral reef in almost total darkness and a heavy sea, and because of his failure to issue timely order to abandon ship when he had nearly half a day in which to prepare for it.

By an ironical twist of fate—almost as if Morrison's prayers had been answered—the lid of "Pandora's Box" came open as the frigate went down. It hit the water and acted as a raft, saving the lives of Heywood, Burkett, Coleman and Larkin, who were able to cling to it.

From the slowly falling hull, as it descended through the green depths, large portions of loose, buoyant wreckage burst free, and went soaring up again towards the surface. Morrison saw a gangway leap out of the waves, almost clear of the water, with Muspratt hanging on to one end. The scene of the sinking was chaotic, drowning, dying men calling in despair for help; but it was every man for himself. "The boats were at some considerable distance in the drift of the tide," wrote Hamilton, "and in about half an hour, or a little better, picked up the remainder of our wretched crew."

Some two-and-a-half to three miles from *Pandora's* reef was a tiny strip of sand, about thirty paces long at high water, which, after they had been assembled there three days, the survivors called "Wreck Reef", or "Wreck Island". On it were clustered eighty-nine men from the *Pandora,* and, still under armed guard, the ten surviving prisoners from the *Bounty.* "The heat of the sun, and the reflection from the sand, was now excruciating," wrote Hamilton. Tents, made of sailcloth, were put up to protect the officers and men of the sunken frigate, but the wretched men of the *Bounty* were refused the use even of an old spare sail; and they had the prison pallor on them. "We had to bury ourselves up to the neck in the burning sand," wrote Heywood, "which scorched the skin (we being quite naked) entirely off our bodies, as if dipped in large tubs of boiling water." "We had our skin flea'd off from head to foot," testified Morrison. Food and water was very short, so short that no water at all was issued during their first day on "Wreck Reef." One man from the *Pandora,* mad with thirst, drank seawater, and died later in consequence. The inimitable Edwards had neglected to stock his four boats. To see if anything could be salved from the wreck, he sent off the master, George Passmore, in one of the boats. He found the topgallant masthead still protruding from the Pacific, and on it—mewing desperately—the ship's cat. The poor beast, terrified by the waste of water lashing at its feet, leaped into the boat, and Passmore brought it back with him to "Wreck Reef".

On August 31 they set out to cover the 1,100 miles that lay between them and Timor, following near to the track of Bligh in the *Bounty's* launch, suffering the same experiences and the same hardships. One note by Surgeon Hamilton has a bearing on the vicious quarrels that developed between Lieutenant Bligh on the one hand and the middle-aged Fryer, Purcell and Cole on the other. "We found old people suffer much more than those that were young"; and, referring to the whole crew, "as their sufferings continued, they became very cross and savage in their temper." Then he refers to Morrison, although not by name. "In the Captain's boat, one of the prisoners took to praying, and they gathered round him with much attention and seeming devotion. But the Captain suspecting the purity of his doctrines, and unwilling he should make a monopoly of the business, gave prayers himself." Hamilton was not in Edwards' boat, and on September 9, merely noticed that "we passed a great many of the Nautilus fish."

But on that day, wrote Morrison, "as I was laying on the oars talking to McIntosh, Captn. Edwards ordered me aft, and without assigning any cause ordered me to be pinnioned with a cord and lash'd down in the boat's bottom, and Ellison, who was then asleep in the boat's bottom was ordered to the same punishment. I attempted to reason and enquire what I had now done to be thus cruelly treated, urging the distress'd situation of the whole, but received for answer, 'Silence, you murdering villain, are you not a prisoner? You piratical dog, what better treatment do you expect?' I then told him that it was a disgrace to the captain of a British man of war to treat a prisoner in such an inhuman manner, upon which he started up in a violent rage and snatching a pistol which lay in the stern sheets threatened to shoot me. I still attempted to speak, when he swore 'by God, if you speak another word I'll heave the log with you,' and finding that he would hear no reason and my mouth being parch'd so that I could scarce move my tongue, I was forced to be silent and submit; and was tyed down so that I could not move. In this miserable situation Ellison and I remain'd for the rest of the passage, nor was McIntosh suffered to come near or speak to either of us."

On September 15, 1791, the four salt-stained boats of the *Pandora* came limping into Coupang, on the island of Timor, just as Bligh's launch had done more than two years before. Edwards' men had been decked out in bright colours, blue and red—the captain was nothing if not a man for the "bull" —but they were very shabby now. The *Bounty's* men were hauled out of them and put into a Dutch jail, where they were soon joined by the survivors of another open boat voyage—ten convicts, including a woman and two children. These prisoners had escaped from New South Wales and reached Timor without any loss of life, after sailing 3,254 miles in 69 days—eclipsing Bligh's record for duration but not for distance. The Dutch at Timor had believed them to be shipwrecked sailors, until Edwards exposed them. The full irony of that strange meeting lay in the fact that the female leader of the convicts—Mary Bryant, a smuggler's girl friend—had first conceived the idea of escaping by sea when she had learned of Bligh's open boat voyage. Now, she found herself imprisoned with some of the *Bounty's* crew; and eventually returned to England with them.

They all embarked in a Dutch East Indiaman bound for Batavia. They passed on the way three pirate prows, then, coasting past Java, came to anchor at Samarang. And there, lying snugly moored, was the schooner Morrison had built, the *Resolution,* lost from sight long ago in a gale. Her crew were in prison, the Dutch Governor having been supplied with a copy of Bligh's "Description List of the Pirates", and suspecting them of being *Bounty* mutineers. Their voyage had been much longer than that of the men in the *Pandora's* boats; in the course of it they had explored the then practically unknown Fiji Islands, and had actually landed on a number of them aided by blunderbusses and some seven-barrelled weapons, in meeting the inevitable rush by screaming cannibals. Their attackers had, quite literally, not known what had hit them, the survivors coming on undeterred by the fact that some of their number were inexplicably falling down.

All the way to the Cape of Good Hope, Edwards and his bullying First Lieutenant, Larkin, continued to confine and ill-treat the *Bounty's* men mercilessly; they were glad to be transferred at the Cape to H.M.S. *Gorgon,* 44 guns. They were now given better rations, allowed up on deck, and secured only by a single leg-iron; Morrison was pathetically grateful to an officer who "very humanely gave us a sail to lay on, which by us was thought a luxury." In his long confinement, to relieve the desperate tedium of the empty hours, Peter Heywood had learned how to make straw hats, with both hands in fetters. These he sold for half-a-crown each and so was able to buy himself a suit of coarse clothes for his homecoming.

On June 18, 1792, there in front of them lay the so familiar —and now so strange—anchorage of Spithead; the tangled greens and browns of Hampshire fields and woods; and a soft English summer sky instead of the bold, brassy sunlight of the Pacific. But still, they were prisoners, awaiting trial for an offence for which there was only one penalty—death.

The *Bounty's* men were transferred to H.M.S. *Hector* to wait out their time—it was to be three months—before the court martial could be convened. But here was a different atmosphere altogether. "We were treated," wrote Morrison, "in a manner that renders the humanity of her captain and officers much honour, and had beds given to us and every indulgence that our circumstances would admit of allowed."

13
"*Dreadful to the Subject and Fatal to Me*"

THE reason for the delay in holding the court martial was that the chief witness was absent. Bligh—he was now Captain Bligh—was away in the South Seas on a second, and successful, breadfruit expedition. He had sailed a year previously and had recently, unknown to him and to everyone else, passed close to the island of refuge chosen by the chief mutineer, Fletcher Christian. If the trial was held at once then both the senior actors in the drama would be unable to testify; on the other hand, it would be inhuman to keep the ten prisoners under threat of death for a period possibly of years. The decision was finally taken to proceed, using Bligh's official reports as the main evidence for the prosecution, backed by the testimony of the survivors of Bligh's boat voyage. It was not strictly justice, but it was merciful. There had, moreover, been a very great change in public opinion.

When Bligh, most anxious that his career and reputation should not suffer from the stigma of losing his ship to a handful of mutineers, had arrived at Portsmouth in March 1790, he had thrilled with pleasure at his unexpected welcome as a national hero. The Royalty Theatre, in May 1790, had put Bligh at the top of the bill, with an ingeniously mounted documentary entitled "THE PIRATES: or, The Calamities of Capt. Bligh". Judging by the playbill, the production budget was a good deal higher than for an equivalent TV show today. The scenes included: "The *Bounty* falling down the River Thames; The Captain's Reception at Otaheite, and exchanging the British Manufactures for the Bread-Fruit Trees; with an Otaheitean Dance; The Attachment of the Otaheitean Women to, and their Distress at parting from, the British Sailors; The Seisure of Capt. Bligh, in the Cabin of the *Bounty*, by the Pirates; With the affecting Scene of forcing the Captain and his faithful Followers into the Boat; Their Distress at Sea, and Repulse by the Natives of one of the Friendly Islands; Their miraculous Arrival at the Cape of Good Hope, and their friendly Reception by the Governor; Dances and Ceremonies of the Hottentots on their Departure; and their happy Arrival in England." To make clear that this was an authentic reconstruction of the actual events—sexy dances and all—the management added: "Rehearsed under the immediate Instruction of a Person who was on-board the *Bounty*, Store-Ship." Such had been the public image projected with all the resources of communication the century could muster; Bligh, however much he may have deprecated it to his friends, must have glowed with pleasure. It was *his* story; the story of the *Bounty* as he had told it. When his book was published, with Admiralty approval and support, the following month, the detailed accuracy of the narrative went unquestioned.

But not now.

Now, two years later, in the summer of 1792, a reversal was under way which, by the time Bligh returned in August, 1793, was complete. Officers who had been associated with the *Bounty's* captain were denied promotion because of it, whereas originally, anyone who had not gone with Bligh in the launch was automatically judged guilty of mutiny and piracy. That was still to be the legal basis of the prosecution's case at the court martial, but the members of the court were going to listen to the evidence sympathetically, instead of condemning out of hand, as Edwards had done. And the author of this violent swing, both in public and in informed opinion, was William Bligh. Bligh—and his blazing temper, that "passionate" nature which made him scream with fury, blind to its effects. He could do it even on paper. And that is exactly what had undone him.

In March, 1790, Mrs. Heywood had written to Lieutenant Bligh to enquire what had happened to her son. Her husband had died two months before and now, on top of that calamity she had learned, by vague report only, that there had been a mutiny in the *Bounty* and that her son's captain had just arrived in England. Heywood was virtually a schoolboy, having joined the Navy when he was just under fifteen, and would have been sixteen at the time of the mutiny. She did not know what had happened. She pictured her boy helpless in the midst of bloodshed and death. The instant reply the agitated woman got from Bligh was appalling in its callousness:

"Madam,

I received your letter this day, and feel for you very much, being perfectly sensible of the extreme distress you must suffer from the conduct of your son Peter. His baseness is beyond all description, but I hope you endeavour to prevent the loss of him, heavy as the misfortune is, from afflicting you too severely. I imagine he is, with the rest of the mutineers, returned to Otaheite.

I am, Madame,

WM. BLIGH."

The cold insinuation, that Bligh hoped and expected that young Peter would hang, was expressed even more clearly by Bligh in a letter to Heywood's uncle, Colonel Holwell:

"Sir,

I have just this instant received your letter. With much concern I inform you that your nephew, Peter Heywood, is among the mutineers. His ingratitude to me is of the blackest dye, for I was a father to him in every respect, and he never once had an angry word from me through the whole course of the voyage, as his conduct always gave me much pleasure and satisfaction. I very much regret that so much baseness formed the character of a young man I had a real regard for, and it will give me much pleasure to hear that his friends can bear the loss of him without much concern.

I am, Sir, &c.,

WM. BLIGH."

That, in both cases, Bligh replied instantly, suggests that he was in a paroxysm of fury, boiling over to lash out and hurt; that it was a long-standing hate, is shown by a private letter written to his wife Betsy before he had even returned to England: "Besides this Villain Christian see young Heywood one of the ringleaders, & beside him see Stewart joined with him . . . I have now reason to curse the day I ever knew a Christian or a Heywood or indeed a Manksman." There, in part at least, is the almost certain explanation of the savage conduct of Captain Edwards towards his prisoners. He must have been briefed by Bligh, in such terms as these, before he sailed in the *Pandora*. It is an obvious conclusion because, while Edwards was fitting out his ship at Chatham, Bligh was on leave at his home in London not many miles away. But what did Bligh have against Heywood? That was the question that puzzled and alarmed the midshipman's family, especially his sister, Nessy, who fought like a tigress for the boy. Shocked and shaken by Bligh's verbal slap in the face, they sought to discover what lay behind the grudge.

They wrote to various people all over the world, to find out what had happened during the mutiny. And the news was black. When they eventually contacted Hallet, "that little wretch", as the furious Nessy called him, wrote that Heywood had sided "with the criminal party", but gave no details, except that he would testify against him. For two years, the family was in a state of dread. All their friends, knowing as little as they, shook their heads gravely and warned them to expect only the worst.

The actual formulation of the charges for the court martial came as a relief: here, they could act in advance of the trial. Another of Heywood's uncles was a serving officer—Commodore T. Pasley. He was in a position to get inside information, and he duly reported to Nessy: "I have seen all the principal evidences, which has occupied my whole thoughts and time. I have no doubt of the truth of your brother's narrative; the master, boatswain, gunner, and carpenter, late of the *Bounty,* I have seen, and have the pleasure to assure you that they are all favourable, and corroborate what he says. That *fellow,* Captain Edwards, whose inhuman rigor of confinement I shall never forget, I have likewise seen; he cannot deny that Peter avowed himself late of the *Bounty* when he came voluntarily aboard. I have been at the Admiralty, and read over all the depositions taken and sent home by Bligh and his officers from Batavia, likewise the court-martial on himself; in none of which appears any thing against Peter." This was true; Bligh had not offered any evidence against Heywood—there was none to give. What then had he against Heywood? Whatever it was, he would not now be able to state it, being still in the South Seas.

Nevertheless, warned Pasley, "I will not deceive you, my dear Nessy; however favourable circumstances may appear, our martial law is severe; by the tenour of it, the man who stands neuter is equally guilty with him who lifts his arm against his captain in such cases." And he recommended that instead of employing eminent counsel for the defence, which the frantic mother of the boy had suggested, a friend of his with great experience as judge advocate at naval courts martial should be employed. Pasley knew that, to put it bluntly, "sea-officers" were averse to lawyers. That was shrewd, but he had at least one friend who was to be a member of the court

—Captain George Montagu of H.M.S. *Hector,* whose humanity in dealing with the prisoners had so impressed Morrison. The fact was, that although the Navy possessed officers like Bligh and Edwards, the majority of naval officers were much as they are now; the ships were less complicated and there were fewer gadgets, but the general atmosphere, as shown in memoirs written at the time, was almost startlingly the same. And it was this body of decent, humane men who were behind Pasley.

An ex-judge advocate then, was to defend Heywood. Muspratt was to be defended by a shrewd local lawyer, Stephen Barney, of Portsmouth. Many of the other prisoners had help of some kind, in preparing their cases—which was virtually all a lawyer could do under the rules of a court martial. Morrison would defend himself.

And, in effect, Christian was to be defended, too. His brother, Edward Christian, Fellow of St. John's College, Cambridge, and Downing Professor of Laws, at that time Professor of Laws in the East India College, Hertfordshire, and later Chief Justice of Ely and editor of Blackstone's *Commentaries,* was to be present, holding a watching brief for the absent mutineer. The anti-Bligh faction was gathering its forces. It was the absence of such support for himself which had caused the lowly-born Fryer to back down and "beg pardon" of Bligh. These people did not mean to defy the ex-captain of the *Bounty;* they intended to break him.

The Court Martial began on September 12, aboard H.M.S. *Duke,* moored in Portsmouth Harbour, and lasted until September 18, under the presidency of Lord Hood, the "Commander-in-Chief of His Majesty's Ships and Vessels at Portsmouth and Spithead." The court was not assembled to find the reaon for the mutiny, but to decide who were the mutineers. Seventeen men of the *Bounty's* crew gave detailed, voluminous, scattered, but not too contradictory, testimony. The trial attracted an enormous amount of attention and many influential visitors; some were present throughout. One of these was the Attorney-General, who left no public record of what he thought about it. Another, Sir Andrew Snape Hamond, captain of the *Brunswick,* and a member of the court, published anonymously his account of the trial in the *Gentleman's Magazine* for December, 1792. His report tells us what the Minutes cannot convey—the atmosphere of the scene, the characters of the accused, and the differing impressions they made.

There was no real case against Norman, Coleman, and McIntosh. Bligh had stated, in the documents before the court, that they had been detained in the *Bounty* against their will. Byrn could prove that he had tried to get into the cutter, but his defence had to be read for him by the judge advocate, for obvious reasons. It began, most movingly and effectively: "It has pleased the Almighty, amongst the Events of his unsearchable Providence, nearly to deprive me of Sight, which often puts it out of my Power to carry the Intentions of my Mind into Execution." After that, there was no chance of Byrn being hanged, either.

Ellison, Burkett, Millward, and Muspratt, on the other hand, were in deadly danger. Young Ellison had been seen under arms by many witnesses, and Hayward said he had run up to Bligh, shouting, "Damn him, I'll be sentry over him." Burkett had actually been one of the men who had entered Bligh's cabin with Christian, according to Bligh, Fryer, and Hayward; and all the witnesses had seen him armed on deck. His defence, that he had been forced to do it "by threats of immediate death," seemed lame. Millward had been an armed sentry over Fryer, but had seemed friendly. He also claimed to have had a weapon thrust into his hands; various pieces of evidence showed it might have been true in his case. Muspratt had been seen by Hayward, so Hayward claimed, under arms within ten minutes after the mutiny had begun; Cole, too, had seen him armed. Muspratt admitted having taken up a musket for a moment, but claimed that he had intended to retake the ship, having been told by Millward of Fryer's abortive "push".

The two doubtful cases—doubtful, that is, under the stern law that to do nothing during a mutiny was to aid the mutineers by default—were Heywood and Morrison.

Fryer deposed that he had not seen Heywood on deck at the seizure of the ship. Cole said he had seen him on deck later, but that the midshipman had then been ordered below by the mutineers; Purcell said he had seen Heywood on deck, looking confused. He had seemed to drop his hand idly on a cutlass, and that he, Purcell, had said—"In the name of God, Peter, what do you do with that?" Purcell was closely questioned, but said he did not believe Heywood was in sympathy with the mutineers. He had taken his hand off the cutlass as soon as Purcell spoke apparently, not realizing until then what might be read into the gesture. Lieutenant Hayward was then called. He said that he had seen Heywood unarmed on deck; that he had later told Heywood to go into the boat, when both of them were below; that he did not think Heywood was prevented from going on deck; that he "rather supposed" Heywood was on the side of the mutineers, but that this must be understood "only as an opinion," as Heywood "was not in the least employed during the active part of it."

The really deadly evidence came from Lieutenant Hallet. He had seen Heywood on deck, not armed, not doing anything, merely "standing still, looking attentively towards Captain Bligh." Then Hallet made his damning statement, which may well have been true: "Captain Bligh said something to him, but what I did not hear, upon which he [Heywood] laughed, turned round, and walked away. Mr. Bligh was then standing with his arms tied behind his back—Christian holding the cord with one hand and bayonet to his breast with the other." Hallet might have added, but did not, that Bligh was dressed only in a night shirt, and was raving mad with impotent fury. Remembering how grossly he had abused Christian—and all the other officers—not so many hours before, any high-spirited lad might well be forgiven for an amused reaction. But it looked as if Heywood might die for laughing.

And if this is what had really happened, then it can be readily understood that the egocentric Bligh would never have forgiven or forgotten.

The warrant officers and petty officers, giving evidence for the prosecution, came to Heywood's aid, however; apparently he was popular. Messrs. Hayward and Hallet were not. Cole on being recalled, testified that both of them seemed "alarmed." Purcell, on being recalled, deposed that both of them appeared "to be very much confused." Precisely what they meant was made quite clear by Burkett, when he was called to defend himself. He described Hayward and Hallet tearfully pleading with Christian *not* to send them away in the boat with Bligh. Ellison confirmed it, adding that when the "two gentlemen rec'd the order they weep't bitterly." Their reactions, when the same story of blue funk was told by four witnesses in a trial that was enthralling all England, must have been interesting. We know that Hallet's father was present, and that he was very bitter against Fryer in particular; he told Bligh afterwards that "he heard some of the captains or gentlemen who were present declare, that the master deserved hanging as much as any of the mutineers." But Anne Hallet was the bosom friend of Betsy Bligh. The factions had already formed; the court martial was their first battlefield; only a spectator could give a disinterested verdict now.

Such a spectator was Sir Andrew Snape Hamond, of H.M.S. *Brunswick,* the senior captain serving on the court martial. But even he was not quite disinterested, for those who were condemned by the court might be placed in his charge, and he would be present at their execution. Knowing this, it was with a more than ordinary interest that he studied the prisoners, and followed their shifting fortunes day by day to the end. It was the boatswain's mate, Morrison, who impressed him above all of the *Bounty's* men.

"This ship," the officer wrote, "appears to have abounded with men above the common herd of uniformed illiterates. The boatswain's mate stood his own counsel, questioned all the evidences, and in a manner so arranged and pertinent, that the spectators waited with impatience for his turn to call on them, and listened with attention and delight during the discussion. Millward, one of the poor fellows who suffered, was also a man of education and capacity. I (later) heard him read Dodd's Sermon to his fellow prisoners, and in such a manner, that, until I saw Millward in the act, I was firmly persuaded one of the chaplains was in performance of his office."

On September 18, 1782, read the Minutes, "the Court was cleared and agreed that the Charges had been proved against the said Peter Heywood, James Morrison, Thomas Ellison, Thomas Burkitt, John Millward and William Muspratt, and did adjudge them and each of them to suffer Death by being hanged by the Neck."

"I was struck with horror and astonishment at hearing them [Heywood and Morrison] being included in the sentence of condemnation," wrote the officer of the *Brunswick*, "as was every one in the Court. Indeed, so very slender were the evidences in favour of the prosecution, that they really did not amount to crimination."

But, the Minutes go on, "the Court, in Consideration of various Circumstances, did humbly and most earnestly recommend the said Peter Heywood and James Morrison to His Majesty's Royal Mercy." There must have been a sigh of relief as that was announced. As expected, Norman, Coleman,

McIntosh and Byrn were acquitted. Ellison, Burkett, Millward, and Muspratt were to die. But Muspratt's Portsmouth lawyer had a final card to play. It was a technical point—that, as all the prisoners had been tried together, and so could not give evidence for each other, Muspratt had been unable to call two of them, Byrn and Norman, who, he stated, would have otherwise been able to give evidence for him. In this, a court martial differed from a trial in the criminal courts. "This Difference, my Lord, is dreadful to the Subject and fatal to me," submitted Muspratt, in a paper read for him by the Judge Advocate.

Mrs. E. Bertie, a friend of Heywood's mother, wrote at once: "I have the happiness of telling you that the court-martial is this moment over, and that I think your son's life is more safe now than it was before his trial. As there was not sufficient proof of his innocence, the Court could not avoid condemning him; but he is so STRONGLY recommended to MERCY, that I am desired to assure you by those who are judges, that his life is *safe* . . ." That also was the verdict of the Attorney-General, given to Heywood's lawyers.

On October 26, the King's pardon for Heywood and Morrison went down to Portsmouth; and Muspratt was acquitted on a point of law. Ellison, Burkett, and Millward, however, were still condemned to die on October 29 aboard H.M.S. *Brunswick,* moored in Portsmouth Harbour. "Great murmurs are carefully breathed, and assiduously promulgated, on the pardon of the midshipman and boatswain's mate," wrote Captain Hamond. "According to the vulgar notion, money bought their lives; and the others fell sacrifices to their poverty."

Then the dreaded order came: the three condemned men were transferred to the H.M.S. *Brunswick.* Captain Hamond wrote: "The evening preceeding the day of execution, the prisoners, under the charge of the provost-martial, escorted by a guard, came on-board. I expected to have seen them emaciated, wan, and half expiring with the keenness of their afflictions; but, to my astonishment, they tripped up and down the ladders with the most wonderful alacrity; and their countenances, instead of being (as I expected) the index of a woeful depression of mind, were perfectly calm, serene, and cheerful. It really gave me a shock to see them, but a few hours before their solemn exit, in the full possession and vigour of their health and spirits, as in seeming ignorance of their approaching fate. Herein I was mistaken, as it was nothing less than a calm resignation, acquired by a length of confinement, and habit of study on religious subjects for some considerable time."

Young Tom Ellison, Burkett and Millward were put into the gunroom and the ports barred. "Not a ray of light was permitted to obtrude. Through a small opening to their cell, I, unperceived, observed them very minutely, heard their conversation, which was cheerful, resigned, and manly. Their faces were the cheerful indexes of serene and placid minds. I never saw them shed a tear."

At ten o'clock of their last night on earth, the three prisoners obediently got into bed; and the provost-martial, who was to hang them by slow strangulation in the morning, retired behind a screen which curtained them off from the rest of the gunroom. In this space, a number of sad, curious, and morbid spectators were gathered. The provost-martial turned to them, and referring to little Tom Ellison, growled. "The young one's a hardened dog." He then pulled a nightcap out of his pocket, and snarled: "Here is one; I have all three of their caps in my pocket." The hangman's obvious relish for his job made the captain of the *Brunswick* curtly order him out of the gunroom. So he went off and had a cheerful drink with the sergeant of Marines.

"At nine o'clock the next morning the fatal gun was fired, and the yellow flag displayed the dreadful summons to claim the attention of the fleet. Boats from every ship asembled, and, in a short time, the ship was crowded within with officers, and men without with boats manned and armed. Along the shore, and even a-float in wherries, were men, women, and children, to the amount of thousands, as if, instead of a solemn scene of sorrow, the hanging were a spectacle of joy. The officers and men were arranged along the deck in columns; the yard ropes stretched along in each man's hand. At eleven the prisoners were summoned up, and marched, preceded by four clergymen, through the ranks of men along the main deck upon the forecastle, when the eternal separation took place between the one who hung on the starboard, and the two who were hung on the larboard, fore yard arms. On the cat-head Millward addressed the ship's company, confessed the errors they had been guilty of, acknowledged the justice of their sentence, and warned them by his fate to shun similar paths of impropriety: his speech was nervous, strong, and eloquent, and delivered in an open and deliberative manner. After half an hour spent in devotion, during which time Morrison performed the last offices to his departing companions, the gun was fired, and their souls took their flight in a cloud, amid the observations of thousands. They behaved with a manly firmness that would have dignified a superior state, merited a better fate, and was the admiration of all!"

They were guilty by the rules of the navy in which they had served, but the real author of their misfortunes, by his conduct, was William Bligh. Admiral Hood, the Commander-in Chief, showed what he thought of Bligh by at once offering Peter Heywood a post as midshipman in the fleet flagship, H.M.S. *Victory*. Edward Christian set to work with Stephen Barney, the Portsmouth lawyer, to produce a transcript of the court martial proceedings, with an *Appendix* giving that part of the evidence which the court had not been able to consider—the reasons for the mutiny. He interviewed Fryer, Hayward, Peckover, Purcell, Smith, Lebogue, Coleman, McIntosh, Heywood, and Muspratt; and corresponded with Morrison. He took great care to have reputable witnesses present at these interviews—they included the Reverend Dr. Fisher, Canon of Windsor, and the Reverend Mr. Antrobus, Chaplain to the Bishop of London. Because the *Bounty's* men were still serving in the Navy, he could not attribute a particular statement to a particular man; but, apart from that, the case he was building up was devastating.

But, before he could publish, Captain Bligh returned in triumph from the South Seas, the breadfruit successfully transplanted, and another "best-selling" book about his experiences maturing in his mind. He found his reception astonishing. The First Lord of the Admiralty, Lord Chatham, refused to see him; but, pointedly, received one of his subordinate officers. The Admiralty said they were not interested in his book, and would not support publication. And, although the nation was now at war, he was put on half-pay and not given a command. In the following year, 1794, Edward Christian's documentary study of the causes of the mutiny in the *Bounty* was published. Bligh immediately published a totally irrelevant reply, and threatened to take legal proceedings. Edward Christian challenged him to do so. For once, the "passionate" Bligh, always ready for a row and the hurling of coarse insults, was strangely silent.

But a full account of the mutiny, from both sides, had still to be written. It was a long time coming and, when it did appear, in 1831, it was by an anonymous author. It attacked Bligh—and Edwards also—in that cold and subtle manner which only authority and inside knowledge could give. The knife was blandly inserted and, when deep enough, turned with precision. The author mentioned Bligh's own "best seller" with a disarming air of fairness. "The story obtained implicit credit; and though Lt. Bligh's character never stood high in the navy for suavity of manners or mildness of manner, he has always been considered as an excellent seaman, and his veracity stood unimpeached." Then, bit by bit, it was impeached, and his character also—"it is well known that his temper was irritable in the extreme." Then the final blast, with all the stops out: "tyrannical conduct, harsh and approbious language, ungovernable passion, and a worrying and harassing temper." It was Bligh to the life. And well it might be, for the author was Sir John Barrow, a former Secretary of the Admiralty. This was Bligh as his contemporaries saw him. J. W. Croker, who followed Barrow as Secretary to the Admiralty, came across a copy of Cook's last published work, in which Bligh had venomously scribbled aspersions against almost every other officer in the ship. Croker noted coolly that it "belonged to William Bligh, who has made some marginal notes, which must be read with grains of allowance for his temper and prejudices."

14
Pitcairn's Island

"It is so high that we saw it at the distance of more than fifteen leagues; and it having been discovered by a young gentleman, son to Major Pitcairn of the Marines, we called it *Pitcairn's Island.*"—CAPTAIN CARTERET, 1767.

IN FEBRUARY, 1808, the American sealer *Topaz* of Boston was in latitude 25°2′S.; longitude 130° W., when the master, Mayhew Folger saw an unnamed island, and steered in towards it in search of seals. The long Pacific swell was breaking in thunder on the rocky base of the island; there was no anchorage. Nevertheless, it was inhabited; columns of smoke from fires were rising above the trees, and there were what looked suspciously like houses perched above the cliffs. As the little Yankee sealer closed in, Captain Folger saw a native canoe come out, incredibly, into the booming surf of that iron-bound shore, and, breaking through the seething water, approach to within a short distance of the ship. Then the canoe stopped, the young men in it seeming nervous of coming too close; they were brown, almost as dark as natives, and dressed in little more than loincloths. At that distance, it was hard to make out what they were saying, but they seemed to want to know who he was. At least, they spoke English. He shouted back that he was an American from Boston.

They began to babble away at him together: "You are an American; you come from America; where is America? Is it in Ireland?"

"Who are you!" Folger roared back at them.

"We are Englishmen."

Totally baffled, Folger shouted: "Where were you born then?"

"On that island which you see."

The Yankee Captain thought that one out, and then called back to them: "How then are you Englishmen, if you were born on that island which the English do not own, and never possessed?"

"We are Englishmen, because our father was an Englishman," came back the reply.

"Who is your father?" roared Folger.

"Aleck," they called. "Aleck."

"Who's Aleck?"

"Don't you know Aleck?" they answered, with disarming simplicity.

"How the h— should I know Aleck?" bawled the Yankee.

"Well then, did you know Captain Bligh, of the *Bounty?*"

And the penny—or the dime—dropped. Folger subsequently told this part of his story, complete with dialogue, to Amasa Delano, master of a whaling ship. The whalers and sealers penetrated not infrequently into this relatively unknown area, hunting down their prey and exploring at the same time, swapping notes with each other. Folger and Delano were well aware of the *Bounty* story, and had often discussed the possible fate of Christian. Now, in Folger's mind, was a "shock of mingled feelings, surprise, wonder, and pleasure, not to be described . . ." He had found the refuge of the mutineers. But there was no sign of the *Bounty* herself.

Eventually, Captain Folger ventured through the surf, and met "Aleck". He was the only white man on the island, although there were thirty-four native or half-English/half-Tahitian youths, women, and children. Aleck then said that he was Alexander Smith, and, in proof of it, gave the American a timepiece and an azimuth compass, which he said had come from the *Bounty*. The other mutineers were all dead, he said; most of them had either murdered each other or been murdered by the natives who had accompanied them there in the *Bounty*, the island itself being uninhabited when they landed.

Folger himself subsequently wrote to a friend: "I stayed with him five or six hours; gave him an account of some things that had happened in the world since he left it, in particular their (Aleck's countrymen's) great naval victories, at which he seemed very much elated, and cried out 'Old England for ever!' In turn, he gave me an account of the mutiny, and the death of his companions."

But the sixty-four dollar question, for Folger, was: what had happened to Christian? Amasa Delano wrote down what his friend Folger told him: "Smith said, and upon this point Captain Folger was very explicit in his enquiry at the time, as well as in his account of it to me, that they lived under Christian's government several years after they landed; that during the whole period they enjoyed tolerable harmony; that Christian became sick and died a natural death; and that it was after this when the Otaheitan men joined in a conspiracy and killed the English husbands of the Otaheitan women, and were by the widows killed in turn on the following night. Smith was thus the only man left upon the island."

Folger reported his discovery, at the first opportunity, to the British authorities; in consequence, on May 14, 1809, the Admiralty in England received a letter from Sir Sidney Smith at Rio de Janeiro, giving the American's story. "The whole population amounts to about thirty-five, who acknowledge Smith as father and commander of them all; they all speak English, and have been educated by him (as Captain Folger represents) in a religious and moral way. Smith gave to Captain Folger a chronometer made by Kendall. Extracted from the log-book of the *Topaz,* 29th Sept., 1808."

There was an Alexander Smith (although his real name was Adams) on the list of the *Bounty's* crew—the court martial had established that he was one of the hard-core mutineers, and that he had stood guard over Bligh with musket and bayonet. The *Bounty's* chronometer had been made by Kendall. The Admiralty quietly filed the information, and did not even notify the captains of warships sent to cruise in the area. Thus it was that Pitcairn was once more "discovered".

In 1814, two British warships, H.M.S. *Briton* (Sir Thomas Staines) and H.M.S. *Tagus* (Captain Pipon), were sent out to the Southern Pacific to hunt down the American raider *Essex.* "On 17th September," reported Staines, "I fell in with an island where none is laid down in the Admiralty or other charts . . ." Folger had given them its position, and told them it was Pitcairn; it really appeared as if the Admiralty did not want to know about the last refuge of the mutineers. Consequently, the two captains, never having heard of Folger, were as surprised as he when a canoe came out to them through the boiling surf, and paddled alongside. A native called up to them from it, in English, "Won't you heave us a rope now?"

And when the first of the young men swarmed up the side and sprang onto the deck, Captain Pipon asked the same astonished question as Captain Folger: "Who are you?"

The youth instantly replied, that he was Thursday October Christian, so called because he was born on a Thursday in October. (Christian seems to have had a rather whimsical attitude to the Tahitians among whom his life had been cast—he called his wife "Mainmast".) Pipon reported that the son of the mutineer had "a countenance extremely open and interesting; spoke English in a manner vastly pleasing; was accompanied by another young man, of the name of George Young, a very fine youth of about 17 or 18 years of age, who also spoke English perfectly well, indeed it was their common and general language." This was the son of Midshipman Young.

Staines and Pipon had some trouble contacting Adams (alias Alexander Smith), who feared he might be hauled home to the hangman, but these two captains had nothing in common with Bligh and Edwards. Pipon wrote: "It would have been an act of the greatest cruelty and inhumanity to have taken him away from his little family, who in such case would have been left to experience the greatest misery and distress, ultimately, in all probability, would have perished of want." But they did want to find out what had happened to the other mutineers—particularly Christian.

It was a story of barbarity and butchery, in which the two thugs, M'Coy and Quintal, had played a leading part; in the end, only these two, plus Adams and Young, were left. All the other men, English and Tahitian, were dead. Then M'Coy, who had worked in a distillery, invented a method of producing spirit from the tree root, brewing it in Quintal's kettle. M'Coy got blind drunk, and fell to his death from a cliff; Quintal went on the rampage among the native women, and was executed by Adams and Young.

The story of how Christian had met his death did not tally with what Adams had said to Folger—but Staines and Pipon were not to know that. To Folger, in 1808, Adams said that Christian had "become sick and died a natural death"; to Staines and Pipon, 1814, he said that Christian had behaved like a tyrant and had very soon been "shot by a black whilst digging in his field". To a later visitor still, Captain Beechy of H.M.S. *Blossom,* who in 1823 had actually been instructed by the Admiralty to inspect Pitcairn, he said that Christian had been killed "working at his yam plot" during the general uprising of the natives, which took place much later. But when asked to point out Christian's grave, he could not do it. Apart from this incident his memory was excellent.

The almost certain reason for these contradictions is that Adams told a lie to Folger in 1808, and having forgotten by 1814 just precisely what the lie had been, blurted out the most likely story that occurred to him. He was subsequently more careful, but not careful enough, slipping up badly on the time sequence. But, if Christian had been killed on Pitcairn and buried there, why should Adams have lied? He would have had a motive only if Christian was still alive. And there is evidence that he was. Evidence that he was in England in 1808, right under the noses of the authorities. Astonishingly, it was an Admiralty official who provided part of that evidence.

In 1808, Peter Heywood—now Captain Heywood, R.N.—was walking down Fore Street, Plymouth Dock, when he realized that a man ahead of him resembled, of all people, his old friend Fletcher Christian—long since vanished in the wastes of the Pacific. The set of the shoulders, the slightly bowed legs, all were the same. Heywood quickened his step; the man ahead, hearing it, half began to run; and then glanced round. It was Christian—it must be! Heywood, too, broke into a run; but the stranger, who was not a stranger, doubling through the back streets, quickly dodged him. Coming to a stop, Heywood wondered what to do. Make further enquiries? But that might be fatal to Christian, and risky for himself. Heywood never did report the incident officially, nor did he mention the matter in any document included in his memoirs. The description of the strange meeting comes from a footnote which Sir John Barrow appended to his book on the *Bounty* mutiny, implying that he personally could vouch for the truth of the story.

In the same year as Heywood's encounter, rumours were circulating in the Lake District, near Christian's home, that the mutineer had returned and was visiting various relatives.

The most persistent reports pointed to an island in Lake Windermere, known as Belle Isle. Later, it became known locally as "Christian's Island", and, during the second world war, when taken over by the Admiralty as a shore establishment, it was renamed H.M.S. Bounty.

It would appear then in tracing Fletcher Christian's history that the year 1808 was a significant one. During those twelve months Folger called at Pitcairn, Heywood thought he saw Christian at Plymouth, and the Lake District rumours of his return became prevalent. It is tempting to connect these events in the above order, and to assume that Folger's ship was the means of escape, but upon close examination such a sequence seems doubtful. For one thing, once the story was about that Christian was back with his family, there would have been strong reason for him to have left the Lake District. When seen in Plymouth, he might well have been, not on his way into England, but on his way out again. In fact, there is no reason to doubt the possibility that Christian escaped Pitcairn long before Folger sighted the island. He could have been picked up by an earlier ship whose movements were not reported, he could have sailed off in a repaired boat from the *Bounty* or he could have built a boat of his own. He had found Pitcairn in the first place although it was hundreds of miles away from the position marked by Carteret, so navigating a course from Pitcairn to the coast of South America would have presented no real problem. There would have been ready cash available in the *Bounty* to finance his journey from there—and the *Bounty's* money was never found.

The only clues we have as to the date of his return to England are literary and they point to around 1795. Wordsworth, the schoolboy friend of Christian, disappeared from public view for various periods between 1795 and 1798, and, in Coleridge's notebook for the same period, there occurs a note for a possible poem: "Adventures of *Christian* the Mutineer". In 1798 the *Lyrical Ballads* were published which included the strange narrative poem *The Rime of the Ancient Mariner.* Coleridge prefixed this apparently rambling fantasy with a prose summary of its story: "How a Ship having passed the Line was driven by Storms to the cold Country towards the South Pole; and how from thence she made her course to the Tropical Latitude of the Great Pacific Ocean; and of the strange things that befell; and in what manner the ancyent Marinere came back to his own Country."

Keeping all the existing evidence in mind, it may be conjectured that the Admiralty's strange failure to take any action about Pitcairn, or even circulate the reports of Folger in 1808 and of Staines and Pipon in 1814, were due to reluctance to reopen the matter at a time when Christian was alive and perhaps in England. They certainly showed mercy to Adams, and, knowing by this time that it was Bligh who had been the real cause of the mutiny, there may have been a preference towards allowing Christian to live out the rest of his life in peace. If this is so, then the despatch of the *Blossom* in 1823 meant that he was dead, and that the Admiralty knew he was dead. Sir John Laughton, the famous naval authority, writing on Christian for the *Dictionary of National Biography,* concluded that the return of Christian to England was "in a high degree probable." It is, at any rate, more believable than Bligh's theory that he captured the *Bounty* merely in order to return to a Tahitian girl.

But Christian did set up the British colony that the surgeon of the *Pandora* had foreseen; and it endures to this day. The grave of the *Bounty* is in Bounty Bay, Pitcairn Island, where she was scuttled at Christian's orders, because her presence above water would betray the refuge of the mutineers. The wreck has been discovered several times, and in 1957 a large anchor was brought to the surface. The *Pandora* lies somewhere near that desolate sandbar called by the survivors, Wreck Island; in 1961 an Australian aqualung diver, Donald Smith, found what he believed to be the remains of the frigate, but was not able to authenticate his find.

As to the other men involved in the now famous mutiny, many of their stories can be traced. In the years following the *Bounty's* voyage, the whole world had gone to war; the great Napoleonic Empire had arisen and been overthrown. Among the millions of dead were some of those who had survived the mutiny, its aftermath and the return to England.

Morrison went down with H.M.S. *Blenheim* off the Isle of Bourbon in 1807. Hallett perished aboard H.M.S. *Penelope*. Hayward, commanding the sloop *Swift,* was destroyed, along with his command, by a typhoon in the China Sea. Fryer, having been refused a character by Bligh, did not suffer noticably from that slight, but went on to reach the top of the tree in his own line, that of navigation, and later commanded several ships; he died in 1817, a few months before Bligh. Peter Heywood died a senior captain in 1831, just before his promotion to Admiral was due. What happened to many of the others is not known, but a friend of the Bligh family once had a drink with old Lawrence Lebogue. "Lebogue," he said, "this is better than being in the boat." "Oh damn me," said the sailmaker, "I never think of the boat."

And Bligh? Bligh went on as he had begun. Specialisation in scientific projects paid off, as he had judged it would—he became a Fellow of the Royal Society, a coveted distinction. Bravery in battle—he had plenty of opportunity for that now, and was line astern of Nelson at Copenhagen in 1801, blazing away at the Danish batteries. But he missed Trafalgar. The issue of the *Hampshire Telegraph* which carried a description of Nelson's last hours on English soil added: "Captain Bligh, appointed Governor of New South Wales, will take his departure in a few days, having received his final instructions." This was a new line of country for Bligh, but he brought the old methods to bear on it. The *Bounty* was long forgotten. He arrived in 1806, and before he had even taken over officially as His Majesty's Captain-General and Commander-in-Chief, he had indulged in a series of dubious land transactions. After he had taken over, he promptly worked his new property with convict labour and stocked it with government cattle, for which it is doubtful if he paid.

Then, meeting an influential sheep farmer named John MacArthur, whom his patron, Sir Joseph Banks did not like, Bligh began to hector the colonial as if he were a seaman—or, for that matter, an officer. "What have I to do with sheep, sir?" he bawled. "What have I to do with your cattle? Are you to have such flocks of sheep and such herds of cattle as no man ever had before? No, sir!"

Sheep farming was then still an experiment, and MacArthur tried to point out that he had had a government recommendation for his project.

"I have heard of your concerns, sir! You have got five thousand acres of land in the finest situation in the country; but by God, sir, you shan't keep it!"

This time he was up against a shrewd Scottish brain and a calm, steely determination. MacArthur was no hot-tempered youngster, who would shed tears of mortification and then take rash and desperate action. He bided his time, he stacked the cards, he manoeuvred Bligh until he had him, surrounded by powerful enemies and blatantly in the wrong. He took a very long time. Then, on January 26, 1808, which happened to be the anniversary of the foundation of New South Wales, he struck. As it happened, Bligh had arrested him; but that made no difference—his plans were laid. That evening, three or four hundred troops of the New South Wales Corps marched up to Government House, flags flying, their band blaring out "The British Grenadiers." Bligh went to ground, and was hauled out from under a bed, by the scruff of his neck, by a burly sergeant of the New South Wales Corps. And they put him on a ship, and sent him home, and got a new governor. Bligh arrived back at Spithead, fresh from his latest mutiny, on October 25, 1810. The report that followed him condemned the two gross faults in Bligh's character—"his longing to gratify his insatiably tyrannic disposition and to advance his pecuniary interest." He never received another appointment, and died on December 6, 1817.

The last man who could remember the *Bounty* mutiny died on March 10, 1834. He was William Purcell—Bligh's old antagonist, the carpenter. Ironically, he spent his last days in Haslar Hospital, on the Gosport side of Portsmouth Harbour, from where he had a clear view out across a mile or so of water to Spithead.

It still looked the same, that grey anchorage, crowded with shipping. No. There was something missing—the masts of the foundered *Royal George* no longer feathered the running tides. The last one had disappeared one night in 1794 after a frigate had rammed it in the darkness. But the hull was still down there, and the dead were in the sea.

AUTHOR'S NOTE

ONE hardly expects survivors, let alone a wealth of testimony, where a mutiny is concerned. The officers, as a rule, are quickly disposed of—murdered and thrown overboard. The mutineers either disappear from sight, or are hanged in short order; in either case they are usually illiterate men. The evidence of what really happened is fragmentary, for the most part concerned with the final outburst of furious emotion and perhaps some act of the captain which immediately preceded the revolt. But of what went before, the long, slow boiling up of temper which culminated in the savage eruption of mutiny, there is scarcely any hint. The amount of documentary evidence from participants and eyewitnesses of the *Bounty* mutiny comes, therefore, as a surprise. But there are a number of good reasons for it.

Chief among these is the fact that the mutiny in the *Bounty* was carried out by educated men. Most of the sailors did not want a senseless butchery, and they had the character to keep the more murderous elements among the mutineers under control. They even had the trappings of power, for their leader, Fletcher Christian, was an officer, recently appointed Acting Lieutenant and second-in-command. The general wish was not to kill Bligh, merely to be rid of him.

In fact, the deposed Bligh was not merely allowed to go

free, but when he asked for some of his books and papers, including the log book of the *Bounty,* his clerk was allowed to fetch them. The ungrateful lieutenant later castigated the mutineers as black-hearted villains, on the grounds that they had neglected to let him have some of his personal notes and charts of past voyages, which were consequently lost forever. But the log of the *Bounty,* which was also Bligh's personal journal of the voyage, went into the boat with him. During the long trip home, he continued to add to it, even making charts of the unknown islands which he passed. Upon his final arrival in England he handed the record over to the Admiralty where, as a State document, it was kept for the statutory period of years before becoming public domain. Eventually it was published as *Log of the Bounty* (Golden Cockerel Press, 1936).*

Although Bligh's unedited day-to-day diary of the voyage is the most important document giving the captain's side of the affair, it is by no means the only account. Bligh wrote a book about his adventures which was first published in 1792, and which reappeared in the 1930's as *Bligh of the Bounty* (Methuen); it is similar to the log, but with the more stringent

---

*Bligh kept a rough log in a 6″ × 4″ pocket book requisitioned from Midshipman Hayward, which he transferred to the Fair Log when the weather and the sea state permitted. However, two revealing entries in the Rough were not included in the Fair. The first: "It is a most unhappy situation to be in a Boat among such discontented People who don't know what to be at, or what is best for them." The second: "Almighty God relieve us from our extreme distress, such as men never felt—conduct us through Thy mercy to safe Haven, and in the end restore us to our disconsolate families and friends." It is normal practice to keep both Rough and Fair logs (I do it myself when running diving operations of historic interest, keeping the Rough in a polythene cover). Bligh's Rough he kept as his own personal souvenir, and it remained in the family after his death in 1817, surfacing only at auction in 1976, when it was bought by the National Library of Australia. As *The Bligh Notebook* a facsimile edition was published in 1986, edited by John Bach. In a note to the *Mariner's Mirror* of November 1987, Björn Sundelius pointed out that Bligh tried to conceal from public knowledge the extent of his navigational equipment during his open-boat voyage, stating that he was not allowed by the mutineers to bring along either the Ramsden sextant or Hamilton Moore's book on navigation, "but the Notebook proves he had both of them". This tends to support Fryer's complaints that Bligh had not told the whole truth regarding the navigation of the launch.

comments edited out. In addition many of his various reports and letters were reprinted in the compendious *Life of Vice-Admiral William Bligh* by George Mackaness (Angus & Robertson, Sydney, 1931) and Bligh's *Answer to Certain Assertions* was preserved and a copy is now held by the British Museum. In 1934 his official *Despatch* to the Admiralty and his *Description List of the Pirates* appeared in a collection of documents entitled *The Voyage of the Bounty's Launch* (Golden Cockerel Press). This book also included the previously private *Journal of John Fryer.*

Fryer, the sailing master of the *Bounty,* did not keep a diary, but he was so incensed by Bligh's one-sided description of the boat voyage; in which Bligh gave all the credit to himself, that he wrote his own version. Since he gave no credit whatever to Bligh, it is best to read Bligh and Fryer together, and then strike a balance. Fryer's *Journal* covers events from just before the mutiny to the arrival of the boat-journey survivors at Batavia. A transcript (now at Greenwich) was preserved in the Royal United Service Institution along with many relics of the mutiny, including Fryer's telescope and the *Bounty's* Chronometer from Pitcairn. The original MS is in the Mitchell Library, Sydney.

In a different category is the *Journal of James Morrison* (Golden Cockerel Press, 1935). Morrison, boatswain's mate of the *Bounty,* kept a diary from beginning to end of the voyage, so that his entries parallel Bligh's until the mutiny, when Bligh and Fryer went away in the launch; Morrison remained in the *Bounty* with the mutineers and recorded what happened thereafter under Christian, at Tahiti, and in the *Pandora.* That this journal, unlike Fryer's, was a day-to-day affair is shown by the fact that dated incidents noted by Bligh in the *Bounty's* log, but nowhere else, occur frequently in Morrison's, and that the dates given are in both cases the same—except for a few discrepancies during the long stay at Tahiti, when Morrison probably wrote up his diary only at intervals. The boatswain's mate could not have had access to Bligh's log, a restricted Admiralty document, and therefore his manuscript must somehow have survived the wreck of the *Pandora;* possibly he gave it for safekeeping to someone who stepped dry into one of the four boats.* An edited version was published by Lady Belcher, a distant relative of Christian, during the campaign against Bligh.

Yet another journal, that of Surgeon Hamilton, was published in 1793 as *A Voyage Round the World in H.M. Frigate Pandora;* it was reprinted, by Francis Edwards, in 1915. This manuscript also survived the wreck of the *Pandora,* as did the ship's log.

Midshipman Heywood, who was with Morrison in the *Bounty* and the *Pandora,* spent part of his time in prison writing a long letter to his mother, describing what had happened to him during and after the mutiny; this letter, with other relevant documents, was published as *A Memoir of the Late Captain Peter Heywood,* R.N., edited by Edward Tagart (Effingham Wilson, 1832).

Still other evidence was elicited at the court martial itself. There, even the stories of those men who were illiterate or inarticulate were taken down, providing a virtually minute-by-minute account of the mutiny. An incomplete transcript of the proceedings was published soon after the trial, based on Stephen Barney's records; the full, official minutes were

* A contrary view is taken Rolf Du Rietz, the modern *Bounty* expert, who in a personal communication to the author in 1988 wrote that "Morrison seems not to have kept a diary in the *Bounty* (but possibly on Tahiti after the mutiny like Heywood's and Stewart's diaries later, lost with the *Pandora*)." He points out that the only original documents now surviving are in the Mitchell Library, Sydney—a brief account written in HMS *Hector* in 1792 and a much longer narrative, also written after his return to England. But rough diaries can survive under the most adverse circumstances, those being kept by POWs in Japanese hands during World War II being a case in point, and a more finished work be later based on them, while the original is mislaid or destroyed, to which my own experiences testify. I also know now, from 30 years' experience of underwater exploration, that paper and writing can survive sea water for periods varying with the type of materials used.

published as *The Court-Martial of the "Bounty" Mutineers,* edited by Owen Rutter (William Hodge, 1931). An eyewitness description of those proceedings, given by Captain Hamond, a member of the Court, was published anonymously in the *Gentlemen's Magazine,* December, 1792.

John Adams, the last of the mutineers to die on Pitcairn, gave his version of the *Bounty*'s story to a number of visiting ship captains. Other friends of Christian also survived to testify to the chief mutineer's own account of his motives and actions, and much of this was used by Christian's family in his defense. Most of these documents are conveniently collected in Mackaness.

Sir John Barrow's semi-official, and at first anonymous, narrative of the mutiny was published, under various titles, in 1831, 1845, 1876, 1886, and 1914; it is brief, but represents the considered official view, and is not favourable to Bligh. The reference to Christian having been seen in Plymouth, after the mutiny, has been followed up by C. S. Wilkinson in his *The Wake of the Bounty* (Cassell, 1953).

Most of these books have either been out of print for a century or more, or were published in the 1930's as limited edition collector's pieces; and I am therefore indebted to the Central Library, Portsmouth, for access to their extensive Naval Collection and for the despatch with which they procured for me those volumes not already on their shelves. I owed them a prior debt, extending over years, for other research into the old sailing Navy and conditions in Portsmouth, the premier naval port at the time of the mutiny.

The descriptions of Old Portsmouth, however, are augmented by the fact that I know the area very well. Until the coming of the Luftwaffe in 1940 and 1941, many of the buildings familiar to the *Bounty's* men were still standing. From my window, at this moment, I can look out across Spithead.

Tahiti I do not know; I borrowed from the descriptions

given by Bligh, Morrison, Hamilton, and their contemporaries, such as Cook, and drawings made by observers such as Tobin.

All in all I found in researching H.M.S. *Bounty* that source material was plentiful. When I took the last page out of the typewriter, I felt a strange sadness; I had come to know them so well, these men of the *Bounty,* from reading what they had themselves written or spoken, that I felt I was saying good-bye to old friends. For Morrison, I had the greatest admiration; but I was half-sorry to say good-bye even to William Bligh, victim at the last of his own unstable temperament.

Alexander McKee, Hayling Island, Hampshire.

ADDITIONAL AUTHOR'S NOTE

When the first Editions in English of this book were published in Britain, 1961, and in the United States, 1962 (French and Danish editions followed later), they came to the attention of Rolf E. Du Rietz of Uppsala in Sweden, who had been a student of the *Bounty* affair since 1949 and has published two important books on the subject, *Studia Bountyana* Vol I (Almquist & Wiksell, Manusprint, Uppsala, 1965), and *Banksia* Vol II (Dahlia Books limited edition, Uppsala, 1981). I was surprised to note that he found that I had "added an original and new and (in the main) absolutely convincing conception of Bligh and of the truth behind the mutiny". It had not been my intention to attempt anything revolutionary. The book had to be written very quickly and so I went to the printed documentary sources and, without preconceptions or taking much notice of what anyone else might have written (let alone a Hollywood scriptwriter!), set down what I found there. Perhaps the fact that I had not been too long in 'civvy street' after ten years in the British Army influenced my views of Bligh.

However, the haste resulted in some minor errors, which Mr Du Rietz pointed out. They have been corrected in this edition. Where he had formed an alternative view, I have either accepted it, or given his interpretation in a footnote. In one case, that of the of the position of Fryer as Master, I have felt necessary to defend my general view by modifying and amplifying what I had originally written. I am most grateful to Mr Du Rietz for his interest and suggestions.

APPENDIX

The *Bounty* was burned at Pitcairn and much broken thereafter while she lay on the seabed. When Luis Marden of the American *National Geographic* magazine found the site in 1957, there did not seem a great deal left. But the *Pandora*, a larger and stronger ship, built for war, seemed a better candidate for partial preservation at least, as she had gone down on the Great Barrier Reef of Australia in deep water and would therefore have been protected to a high degree against stormwave action.

In 1977 a Neptune reconnaissance aircraft of the Royal Australian Air Force was flying a search pattern off northern Queensland, opposite New Guinea. She was a four-engined subhunter, carrying a magnetometer, an instrument which measures changes in the earth's magnetic field caused by say, two or three thousand tons of submarine. Would it find the perhaps 100 tons of metal in the *Pandora*?

The scheme had been devised by Ben Cropp, a famous Australian diver and maker of underwater films, and the naturalist Steve Domm. Their diving boat was anchored near a part of the reef marked on charts as 'Pandora Entrance'. But the magnetometer in the aircraft above gave negative readings until Cropp suggested that the pilot try the seaward side of the reef. At once, he got two contacts, which he marked with smoke candles.

Cropp and Domm drove over in their dive boats, dropped

buoys, and sent divers down. They found nothing. But next morning, Cropp found that his anchor chain was almost on the wreck. The guns and the big, old-fashioned anchors convinced Cropp that this was the *Pandora*, and he radioed the government at Canberra. The result within two days was a message that the site was now legally protected as that of an historic wreck. But positive identification did not come until 1979, through markings on a rudder pintle.

In 1983 the Queensland Museum, South Brisbane, sent a team under Ron Coleman, curator of Maritime History and Archaeology, to survey and excavate the site; and in 1984 Luis Marden visited them and dived to the *Pandora* as he had dived to the *Bounty* all those years before.

The wreck lies at 120–30 feet, in an area of fast currents; when northerly winds set in, the sea is flat as a board, but south-easterlies raise very rough water. To judge by the photographs, underwater visibility can be excellent. The finds so far have included a watch probably belonging to Surgeon Hamilton and a padlock which might have secured the rod and leg irons on an imprisoned seaman from the *Bounty*. Excavation will probably go on for many years. The hull is starboard bow down. There is nothing of the stern remaining, other than intact sheathing.

INDEX